# GET GROWING

# Get Growing

**An Everyday Guide to High-Impact, Low-Fuss Gardens**

## Frankie Flowers

PHOTOGRAPHY BY SHANNON J. ROSS

Collins

*Get Growing*
Text copyright © 2011 by Frank Ferragine. All rights reserved.
Photographs copyright © 2011 by Shannon J. Ross. All rights reserved.

Published by Collins, an imprint of HarperCollins Publishers Ltd

First Edition

All photographs by Shannon J. Ross with the exception of the following:

Courtesy of the Ball Horticultural Company
Browallia on pages 113 and 296 are 'Bells Marine' Browallia; stock on pages 65 and 312 are 'Hot Cakes Mix' Mattiola;
torenia on pages 113 and 313 are 'Clown White Blush' Torenia; viola on pages 65 and 314 are 'Sorbet Coconut Duet XP' Viola;
zinnia on pages 170 and 316 are 'Double Cherry Zahara' Zinnia.

Courtesy of iStockphoto
Page 31, White clover; 44–5, soil; 65, sweet pea; 87, tuberous begonia; 92, candytuft; 102, daphne and oleander;
105, English daisy and hollyhock; 114, tuberous begonia; 168, bleeding heart; 201, cat; 221, squirrel; 279, amaryllis;
293, alyssum 'Mountain Gold' and amaranthus; 297, candytuft and chickweed; 299, crocus; 300, daphne; 301, English daisy;
302, fritillaria and geranium; 303, hollyhock; 306, nannyberry; 307, oleander and oriental poppy; 312, sunburst honey locust;
313, sweet pea and tansy; 314, tuberous begonia; 315, white clover.

Illustrations of USDA Plant Hardiness Zone Map (page 6, top) and Plant Hardiness Zones of Canada (page 6, bottom)
by Mike Del Rizzo. Source: The 2003 US National Arboretum "Web Version" of the USDA Plant Hardiness Zone Map; and
Agriculture & Agri-Food Canada. Plant Hardiness Zones of Canada, 2010. Reproduced with the permission of the Minister
of Public Works and Government Services, 2010.

Illustrations on pages 48, 49, 152, 284, and 285 by Alyce Ferragine. Reproduced by permission of the artist.

Nature Mix logo used by permission of Premier Tech Home & Garden

HarperCollins books may be purchased for educational, business, or sales promotional use
through our Special Markets Department.

HarperCollins Publishers Ltd.
2 Bloor Street East, 20th Floor
Toronto, Ontario, Canada
M4W 1A8

*www.harpercollins.ca*

Library and Archives Canada Cataloguing in Publication data is available upon request

ISBN 978-1-55468-833-3

Printed and bound in Canada
TC 9 8 7 6 5 4 3 2 1

To my boys, Gavin and Matheson.
May your garden of life be weed-free
and full of colour.

I LOVE YOU!

# Contents

GET GROWING

Digging In

So you want to be a gardener. Or maybe you've bought your first home and now you *have* to be a gardener! Either way, this book is designed just for you: *Get Growing* will show you exactly how to create a beautiful garden with a minimum of fuss. It will take you from being a dirt-stained putterer to the envy of your neighbourhood!

If you're feeling intimidated, don't worry—I'll be there to guide you along the way. I've been gardening since the age of two. My first home, in Bradford, Ontario, was connected to a greenhouse. My grandfather came to Canada in 1956 and found work in the Holland Marsh, an agricultural community north of Toronto. He and my father, Tony, later purchased their own land in the area, and in 1975 they opened Bradford Greenhouses, which is now one of the largest grower-retailers in central Ontario. I often joke that my family believed in child labour: the greenhouse was my afterschool program, my Sunday school, and my summer vacation, and I loved every minute of it. With countless customers asking questions and thousands of plant problems to solve—not to mention owning four different homes over the years—I've come to know a bit about gardening, and I want to share that with you.

My grandfather came to Canada in 1956 and eventually bought a tract of farmland. That's him with my father (*above right*) — looks like Dad didn't share my early love of farms!

My great-uncle had his hands full with me as a baby (*top*). But as soon as I was old enough to dig, I was helping out at our family's garden centre.

My dad helped open Bradford Greenhouses in 1975 (*above left*), and you can still find him there today! The business is one of the largest grower-retailers in central Ontario.

common sense. There's also a learning curve that everyone has to follow. I often compare it to cooking: you might start off with instant mac and cheese, move on to pasta with sauce from a jar, and then graduate to making your own sauce from scratch. Eventually, you'll be ready to de-bone and stuff a chicken! In the same way, your confidence will grow, along with the plants in your garden. Like cooking—and life in general—gardening involves a lot of trial and error. I'll do my best to help you keep those errors to a minimum: throughout the book, I'll break things down into easy steps, and that will remove much of the guesswork.

Before you get started on your journey, take some time to get to know your garden—and yourself. Start by reflecting on these questions:

## What do I want to do with my garden?

Any time you start a gardening project, think about your specific goals. Are you looking to completely overhaul your landscape or simply maintain the existing look? Do you want to grow vegetables or just flowers? Do you want to improve the property's curb appeal or just create a place to relax? Do you need a space for children to play? Do you want to block your neighbours' view into the backyard?

## How much time can I invest?

Depending on your ambition, a garden can take an hour a week or it can take over your life! Be realistic: if you have a full-time job,

**N**ow to the realities of gardening. It's hard work—there is no such thing as a maintenance-free garden or plant. You'll get dirty. You'll kill some plants (I still do). But it's a hobby with a huge payoff. Sure, a garden will add curb appeal and raise the value of your home, but if that's all you want, you can hire someone to do the gardening for you. For me the pleasures are more intangible: sitting on the deck and enjoying a yard full of blooms, creating a centrepiece with cut flowers I grew myself, slicing a fresh tomato from my garden. Nothing else compares.

Gardening is not rocket science, but it does require some practical knowledge and kids, a dog, and a busy volunteer schedule, then installing a huge vegetable garden is not a good idea. You're far more likely to enjoy your hobby if you keep your plans manageable. If you've moved into a new home, ask yourself if you can maintain what the previous owner began. If the property includes just a few shrubs and some sorry-looking daisies, you can probably start digging new beds. But if you bought your home from a retired green thumb with no children except his prized azaleas, then your first job may be to scale down the existing gardens.

**How much do I want to spend?**

I suggest creating a garden budget every year. Believe me, once you get hooked on gardening, you'll find yourself wanting to purchase every plant, ornament, and tool you see, and the costs add up quickly. You may want to leave your wallet at home during your first trip to the garden centre: just take some time to look at the prices of perennials, shrubs, soil, mulch, and tools. Make note of these prices and use them to create a budget. If you're doing a major garden reno, I recommend hiring a Certified Landscape Designer, who can create a complete plan and give you cost estimates, whether you'll be doing the work yourself or hiring professionals.

It's important to know your property before getting down and dirty. I find it helpful to take a piece of graph paper and make a sketch. Start by plotting out your lot, including your house, driveway, walkways, deck, shed, and pool. These are known as "hardscape."

Select good-quality tools, but don't get carried away by buying every garden gadget you see.

Next, plot the existing gardens, shade trees, and hedges. If you can identify the mature plants, you'll find it easier to understand the conditions in your garden. For example, if the best performers are hostas, ferns, and astilbe, the area probably doesn't get much sun because all of these plants thrive in shade. I know that, at this point in your gardening career, identifying plants is probably going to be difficult. But you may be able to get help from a friend or neighbour. If not, take a few pictures of the plant, including close-ups of the leaves, stems, and flowers, and bring them to your local garden centre for identification.

If you're not sure what's growing in your garden, snap some photos and ask for help identifying the plants at your garden centre (*top*).

Always start any garden project with a plan. You don't need to be an architect—a rough scale drawing will do just fine (*left*).

# Plant Terms You Need to Know

**annual:** a plant that lives for just one season. Annuals are usually planted to give constant colour during the growing season. They need to be replaced every year. Examples include petunia (*left*), marigold, and impatiens.

**biennial:** a plant that lives for two years. Usually, the plant flowers only in its second year, sets (grows) seeds, and then dies. Many will reseed themselves—that is, the seeds they've grown in the second year fall to the ground and produce new plants the next spring. Examples include foxglove (*left*) and hollyhock.

**perennial:** a plant that can overwinter and come back year after year in your hardiness zone. Examples include coneflower, hosta (*left*), black-eyed Susan, and day lily.

**evergreen:** a plant that keeps its foliage (often needles) throughout the winter. Examples include pine (*left*), cedar, and spruce.

**broadleaf evergreen:** a non-needle plant that holds most of its foliage throughout the winter. Examples include boxwood, euonymus, and rhododendron (*left*).

**deciduous plant:** a tree or shrub that drops its leaves in the fall and grows new leaves in the spring. Examples include maple (*left*), oak, and birch.

# Plant Hardiness Zones of Canada

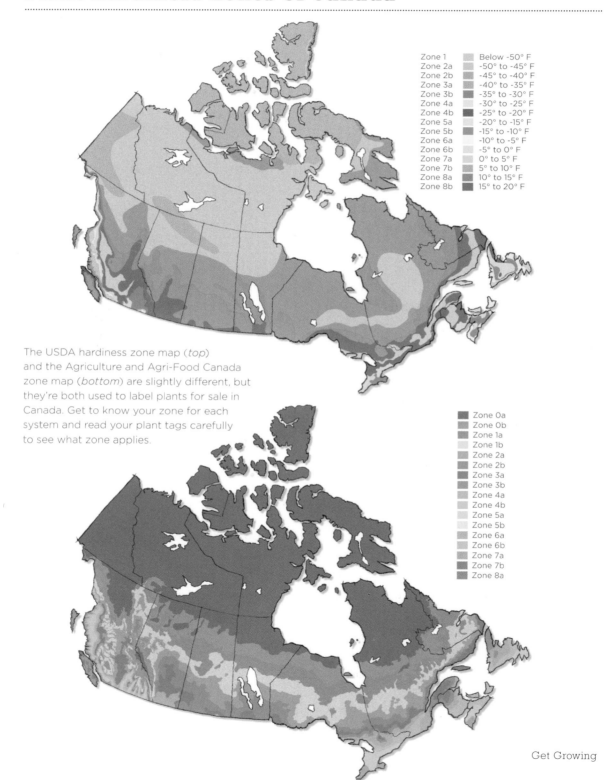

| | | |
|---|---|---|
| Zone 1 | | Below -50° F |
| Zone 2a | | -50° to -45° F |
| Zone 2b | | -45° to -40° F |
| Zone 3a | | -40° to -35° F |
| Zone 3b | | -35° to -30° F |
| Zone 4a | | -30° to -25° F |
| Zone 4b | | -25° to -20° F |
| Zone 5a | | -20° to -15° F |
| Zone 5b | | -15° to -10° F |
| Zone 6a | | -10° to -5° F |
| Zone 6b | | -5° to 0° F |
| Zone 7a | | 0° to 5° F |
| Zone 7b | | 5° to 10° F |
| Zone 8a | | 10° to 15° F |
| Zone 8b | | 15° to 20° F |

The USDA hardiness zone map (*top*) and the Agriculture and Agri-Food Canada zone map (*bottom*) are slightly different, but they're both used to label plants for sale in Canada. Get to know your zone for each system and read your plant tags carefully to see what zone applies.

| | |
|---|---|
| | Zone 0a |
| | Zone 0b |
| | Zone 1a |
| | Zone 1b |
| | Zone 2a |
| | Zone 2b |
| | Zone 3a |
| | Zone 3b |
| | Zone 4a |
| | Zone 4b |
| | Zone 5a |
| | Zone 5b |
| | Zone 6a |
| | Zone 6b |
| | Zone 7a |
| | Zone 7b |
| | Zone 8a |

Get Growing

In the chapters that follow, I'll have lots to say about selecting the right plants for each part of your garden. But for now, let's look at the overall conditions on your property:

# Hardiness Zone

Before you even think about choosing plants, you'll need to know your hardiness zone. Every region of Canada has been assigned a zone number, from 0 to 8, based on its climate. The lower the number, the lower the minimum temperature in that region and the fewer the plants that will survive winter. In other words, a perennial in Chilliwack, British Columbia (Zone 8) may be only an annual in Goose Bay, Labrador (Zone 2)! Staff at your garden centre should be able to tell you what zone your community is in. If not, go to this Agriculture and Agri-Food Canada website (it has a complete plant hardiness zone map): http://atlas.agr.gc.ca/phz.

Whenever you buy a perennial, shrub, or tree, the tag will tell you which zones it will survive in. Unfortunately, this can be a bit confusing. To begin with, many plant tags show the zone map for the United States, which is a bit different from the one used in Canada. For example, my hometown is in Zone 5a according to the Canadian map, but it's in Zone 4b on the U.S. version.

It's important not to take zone maps as gospel: local conditions, such as winds and elevation, can create microclimates that can turn Zone 6 into Zone 4. If you're planting on a patio 10 storeys up, for example, your zone will drop to a lower number. So only buy plants that are labelled as hardy in your zone, but don't blame yourself if something dies over the winter. I always say that the best way to figure out what's truly hardy in your area is to drive around and see what's growing in your neighbours' gardens. If it grows for them, it should grow for you.

# Light

Whenever you buy a plant, the tag will tell you the light conditions it needs:

**Full sun** means six or more hours of direct sun each day. Think of the hottest places on your property—the places where you're most likely to get a sunburn. If your garden receives its most intense sunlight during the hours of 11:00 a.m. and 3:00 p.m., and if it's facing west or south without the shade of a large tree, you can bet you have full sun.

**Partial sun and partial shade** mean more or less the same thing: three to six hours of direct sun. (If the tag specifically mentions "full sun," put the plant in an area that gets hot afternoon sun. If it says "partial shade," give the plant most of its sun in the morning.) Plants in this category may like filtered or "dappled" light, like the light you'd find under a tree with small leaves, such as a locust.

## Frankie's Tip

Hold onto your plant tags for everything in your garden— annual and perennial. They can help you remember exactly what you planted—so you can get it again or avoid it!—and they can remind you of each plant's needs.

7047
9.0327-74
GROWN IN CANADA
CULTIVÉ AU CANADA

**Shade** does not equal darkness. (Only mushrooms will grow in the dark.) Full shade means the plant should have three or fewer hours of direct sun—because many shade plants cannot handle any afternoon sun—and it should spend the remainder of the day in filtered sun or shade.

## Water

Finding the right balance of moisture is key to creating healthy roots and thus a healthy plant. You'll often hear that a plant likes "well-drained soil." This means it likes its share of moisture, but it doesn't want to have wet feet for too long! (This is especially true of indoor plants: too much water is the number 1 reason that houseplants die.) In general, some plants are quite drought tolerant, while others will quickly wither in hot, dry weather.

## Soil

If you were building your dream home, you would build it on a solid foundation. When you're building your dream garden, your foundation is the soil. That's where plants anchor their roots, obtain oxygen, take in moisture, and absorb nutrients. A plant's overall health will be determined by the soil where it's planted. Learning to identify the basic types is key:

**Sand** is made up of coarse particles, so it drains well, but it's lacking in nutrients. Basically, it's like a sieve.

**Silt** is a finer material than sand and often contains some organic matter. It can become very hard and compacted when it dries.

**Clay** is made up of very fine particles of minerals. It retains a lot of moisture, is usually acidic, and doesn't allow for good drainage.

Here's a trick for determining the soil structure on your property. Take an empty Mason jar and remove the lid. Scoop a sample of soil from the middle of your garden (dig down to get a sample from where the roots grow) and place it in the jar. Now fill the jar with water, add a teaspoon of liquid dish soap (this helps separate the soil), screw the lid back on, shake the jar, and let the jar stand for several hours. The soil will settle in layers: sand will settle to the bottom first, as its particles are the heaviest. A darker layer

The soil jar test can help you understand the proportion of sand, silt, and clay in your garden.

of silt will settle on top of the sand, while the light-coloured clay particles will take the longest to eventually settle at the top. By looking at the relative thickness of the layers, you can estimate the proportion of each material that is found in your soil. For example, it might be half sand, one-quarter silt, and one-quarter clay.

If you don't want to go to that much trouble, here's an easier way to determine your soil structure. Grab a handful of soil and squeeze it in the palm of your hand. If the soil runs right out of your hands, you've got a lot of sand. If you can easily mould a cylinder of soil, it's primarily clay. (Too much silt is not typically a problem in garden soil.) What you want is a happy medium: soil that almost clumps together into a cylinder but that falls apart at the last moment.

The ideal garden soil is often called "loam." It's rich in organic matter and contains about two parts sand, two parts silt, and one part clay. If your soil has too much sand or silt, your goal will be to improve moisture retention and add nutrients. You can do this by adding equal amounts of topsoil and peat moss—or by using triple mix (a blend of topsoil, peat moss, and composted manure). The difficulty with sand is that over time, it will always move to the surface, so it will force you to improve your soil continually. Horticultural lime (available at garden centres) will help reduce the acidity of clay, but I've never found anything that will improve its structure. The only lasting solution is to dig it out or build on top of it. I recommend building a raised bed edged with stone or pressure-treated lumber. Dig out as much clay as you can, put down a layer of coarse stone for drainage, and then add your new soil on top.

The reality is that most homeowners will not have rich, loamy soil on their property. They're more likely to have heavy clay or, worse, the dreaded builder's fill, which is just sand and clay mixed with junk like stones, broken bricks, and maybe a few beer cans. If you want a successful garden, improving poor soil like this is a must: clear out as much as possible and replace it with triple mix or good, old compost. In garden lingo, this is called "amending the soil."

## pH

This may sound like Grade 11 chemistry, but all soil can be either acidic or alkaline, and this has a huge impact on a plant's ability to take up certain nutrients. The acidity or alkalinity of your soil is measured on a pH scale that ranges from 0 to 14. Most plants grow best in soil that is neutral, which means it has a pH near 7.0. But plants such as azaleas, rhododendrons, and blueberries need acidic soils (below 6.0) to grow well. Acidic soils are sometimes called "sour." On the other end of the scale is clematis, which enjoys "sweet," or alkaline, soil with a pH of more than 7.0.

How do you know which type of soil you have? As a rule of thumb, soils that contain a lot of clay or peat moss are acidic. Pine needles also add acidity to the soil as they break down, so areas under evergreens usually have a low pH. Adding horticultural lime (available at garden centres) or wood ash from your fireplace can make soil more alkaline.

You can buy soil-testing kits to measure the pH of your garden, but let me be honest: I've rarely tested my soil unless I've seen plants

Sandy soil (*top left*) tends to fall apart in your hands. It offers good drainage, but doesn't retain moisture and contains little or no organic material. Clay soil (*top right*) clumps together when you squeeze it. Clay is the enemy of many suburban gardens: it has poor drainage, and is easily compacted and acidic. Loam (*bottom left*) is rich in organic material and contains a balance of sand, silt, and clay. You can recognize it by feel: it holds its shape briefly when you squeeze it, but eventually breaks apart. Peat moss (*bottom right*) absorbs water like a sponge and loosens compacted soil. It's a great amendment for both sand and clay, as well as the main ingredient in potting soil.

To measure the acidity of soil, you can buy an inexpensive pH test (*left*). You just put a soil sample in the water and drop in the pill: the colour of the water indicates the pH level. The pH here is neutral—good soil to work with.

struggling. For most locations with good soil, you can generally assume the pH will be neutral.

I should stress that you don't need to go through this entire process every time you want to add a plant to your garden. The idea is simply to understand the overall features of your property (make some notes so you don't forget!). Your ultimate goal is to pick the right plant for the right place. Soon you'll be able to put it all together, walk into the garden centre, and announce: "I need a plant that thrives in Zone 5, in shade, and in a dry, sandy soil with a neutral pH."

Now that you've got to know yourself and your garden, it's time to get to know this book! I've organized everything by season, so you don't have to read it cover to cover all at once. Just use it when you need it, and I'll be there to help guide you through the season you're in. I start with helping you prepare the groundwork in early spring and select and plant perennials and annuals a bit later in the spring. Then I show you how to maintain your garden during the ravages of summer, offer tips for enjoying fall colours and a harvest of vegetables, and help you wind down as winter approaches.

Each chapter except the Winter chapter is divided into three sections: Flower Garden (which includes any ornamental plants, whether or not they actually flower), Vegetable Garden, and Lawn. There are a lot of jobs to do each season, so all the sections begin with a check-list that will help you stay organized. (I'm easily distracted, so I like to create to-do lists to keep me focused—although sometimes I spend more time on the list than on the actual tasks!) Feel free to skip over any step that doesn't apply to your situation. After you've finished reading each sec-tion, the checklist will be a handy review: use it to draw up your own to-do list of seasonal jobs.

**Now, let's get growing!**

**Early Spring**

# Getting Ready to Grow

Gardeners look for the signs of early spring like a kid waiting for Christmas. The weather guy in me knows that the first day of the season is March 20, but if you're a gardener, you can't go by the calendar. Wherever you live in Canada, learn to recognize nature's first signs of spring in your area: robins singing, forsythias bursting into bloom, crocuses popping out of the ground—and gardeners hauling their winter-weary bones out of the house!

I like to think of early spring as a season of preparation. It's too early to do much planting, since overnight frost is still likely—I have many memories of tender annuals planted too soon and turning into frozen, fallen friends. At this time of year, you'll concentrate on getting the lawn and garden ready for the warmer weather that's on its way. This means cleaning up, re-pairing winter damage, digging new beds, and amending the soil so you'll be ready to go when it's planting time. In fact, early spring may be the busiest season in the garden, so it helps to be organized. Remember to use those checklists!

# LAWN

**Your early-spring lawn checklist:**

✔ Decide whether you need to replace entire sections of your lawn, and prepare these areas for seed or sod as necessary.

✔ Lightly rake your lawn to remove excess thatch.

✔ Repair areas that were damaged over the winter.

✔ Aerate your lawn to allow water, oxygen, and nutrients to penetrate the roots.

✔ Thicken sparse areas by top-dressing and overseeding.

✔ Give the grass a light mowing.

✔ Feed your lawn with a nitrogen-rich fertilizer.

✔ Use a weed preventer (corn gluten) to deter crabgrass.

In the other chapters of this book, I'll discuss the flower and vegetable gardens before we get to the lawn. But in early spring, there's not much to do in the garden. Your grass, on the other hand, will be in need of repair and rejuvenation. Just be careful not to start too soon. When you walk around your property, does the ground feel spongy? If so, wait before beginning your lawn work. Walking on soggy ground will compact the soil and may even damage your grass.

*Laying sod is hard work. I may be smiling now, but I'll be huffing and puffing soon enough!*

*Get Growing*

Your lawn may look like a battlefield in early spring! If it's beyond repair, you may need to start from scratch with seed or sod.

Once the ground is firm under your feet, take some time to remove leaves, fallen branches, and any other debris from the lawn. A matting of leaves over one area can do a lot of damage: it will block out much-needed light and eventually suffocate and kill your grass.

## Starting a Lawn from Scratch

**N**ow that you've cleared it off, take a second to stand back and survey your yard. A blanket of snow can hide a lot of lawn woes! If your lawn looks like a battlefield in early spring, you may be better off simply replacing it. I use the 50/50 rule: if your lawn is 50 per cent damaged, you're better off starting over, rather than trying to fix it. Once you add up the time and money spent on seed, soil, and fertilizer, it's likely cheaper and quicker to start from scratch.

If less than 50 per cent of your lawn is damaged, congrats! You can skip this section and move on to the steps to get it looking even better. But if things are looking a little rough, you have two choices when growing a new lawn: seed or sod. Seed is a lot cheaper, but it takes more time. Laying new sod gives you a great-looking lawn immediately, but it's expensive. Depending on the type and quality of seed you choose, a lawn measuring 465 square metres (5,000 square feet) will cost you $75 to $100 for seed and fertilizer. Covering the same area with sod will cost 10 to 15 times more, even if you do the labour yourself!

The steps for prepping your lawn are essentially the same for both seed and sod:

1. Start with a bare canvas. That means you'll have to strip out the old turf. If you have a small lawn, you can probably do this yourself by renting a Rototiller. For large areas, however, you're better off hiring a professional, who will also make sure the grade slopes away from the house and not toward it.

2. Add a layer of good topsoil. 10 to 20 cm (4 to 8 inches) is ideal, but just do the best you can. Mixing this into the subsoil will improve drainage and provide more organic matter to support the lawn's roots.

3. Rake, level, and lightly roll the soil. For small lawns, you can use a large hand roller (it looks like a barrel with a big handle, and you fill it with water to supply the weight) or for larger properties you can buy or rent a bigger version that you pull behind a lawn tractor or ATV.

4. Apply a seed-and-sod starter fertilizer. These are high in phosphorus to encourage strong root development.

## Growing from Seed

The best time to apply grass seed is when the temperature is no cooler than 15°C (59°F). While you can get a jump start on preparing your new lawn in early spring, your seed will not germinate until soil temperatures warm up.

When you're buying grass seed, check the label and choose a mixture with a high percentage of ryegrass and fescue and a low proportion (less than 20 per cent) of Kentucky bluegrass. Kentucky blue may look good, but ryes and fescues are tougher: they require less water and are more disease resistant. Some grass seed mixes are specifically designed for hot, sunny areas, while others are better for shade, so choose the one that suits your location.

Buying in bulk is generally cheapest, but don't focus only on price: bargain grass seed will typically have low germination rates. Coverage also varies, so check the bag or ask the garden centre for help.

You can broadcast (scatter) grass seed with a spreader or even by hand if you're trying to cover a small area. Try to achieve even coverage. You don't need to coat the entire surface of lawn, but be generous: think of poppy seeds on a bagel. I like to reapply grass seed every two or three weeks until the area is full and thick. Grass seed doesn't need to be covered, but it does need to make contact with the soil. You can help by lightly going over the area with a fan rake or even with a light rolling. Make sure the seed isn't buried more than 7 mm (1/4 inch) deep.

### Frankie's Tip

It's hard to estimate how much soil you'll need to cover an area. When you're ready to order your soil, measure the length and width of your lawn: any reputable soil supplier should be able to determine exactly how much you need to cover that area to your required depth.

2047
9.0327-74

GROWN IN CANADA
CULTIVÉ AU CANADA

*Get Growing*

Once you've seeded the area, follow these tips to ensure good results:

1. Keep the area moist: do not allow the seed to dry out. I generally like to seed a lawn just before a period of rain, but if you need to water, morning is best. The goal is to keep the first few centimetres of soil moist but not flooded. If the weather is dry, you'll need to water daily—or even a couple of times a day—for the first three or four days.

2. Stay off the area until the new grass is established.

3. Do not use any weed control—natural or chemical. Corn gluten, for example, will prevent crabgrass from growing, but it will also stop the grass seed from germinating.

4. Do not mow until the grass is 8 to 10 cm (3 to 4 inches) high.

5. Do not use high-nitrogen fertilizer until the lawn is well established: for the first season, you want to focus on strong roots, not top growth.

6. If your new lawn still has sparse or bare patches, continue to overseed every 10 days or so: unlike my hair, your lawn can get thicker!

After spreading grass seed, rake the area to give the seed a light covering of topsoil.

# Laying Sod

Sod isn't always available in early spring: if it's cold and the snow is late to leave, you won't be able to find it. However, if Mother Nature turns up the heat a bit, early spring may be the perfect time of year to lay sod.

How much do you need? The size of a roll can vary, but the standard size is 9 square feet (about 1 square metre). So it's time for some simple math: measure the length and width of your property and multiply to find the area. (If the space is irregular, divide it into smaller sections and add the areas together.) Once you determine the square footage, divide by nine to figure out the number of standard rolls you need.

When your sod is delivered, remember that it's perishable: if you leave it exposed for too long, it will die. Try to time your delivery so the sod arrives the same day you plan to install it. If this isn't possible, place the sod in a shaded location.

Prepare the site the same way you would if you were seeding (see above). Then get ready to roll! Be warned: laying sod is tough work, so ask a friend or two for help.

Use your driveway, property line, or sidewalk as a guideline to follow as you lay your sod. Stagger the rows, laying the sod in a brickwork pattern. That is, make sure that when you lay down the second row, the middle of each piece of sod lies against the lines between pieces in the first row. Then lay the third row against the second row in the same way—and so on. (When laying sod on a slope, start at the bottom and lay the rows horizontally, not from the bottom to the top. For steep slopes, you may need to drive a thin stake through the middle of each piece to stop it from sliding down the slope.) The edges of the sod should butt right up against each other: don't overlap the pieces or leave spaces between them. If some spaces are smaller than the size of one piece of sod, cut the sod to size, using a sharp knife or spade. When you're done, roll the entire area to remove air pockets and to make sure the roots have made contact with the soil.

Water your new sod immediately and generously. Make sure the water penetrates the sod and reaches the soil line: that's at least 2.5 cm (1 inch) of water. Sod needs to be kept moist until it's established. The frequency of watering depends on the weather and soil type: it could be as little as once a week or as often as daily. You can lay off on the water once the sod has established itself—you'll know it's taken root when you can no longer lift a piece off the ground.

Keep off a newly sodded area for as long as possible: walking on it will compact the soil, and if the sod has just been watered, you may even create footprints and uneven patches. A newly sodded lawn can be mowed in as little as seven days, but don't cut it too short: leave it about 8 cm (3 inches) long. And always keep your blade sharp.

Lay off the herbicides or nitrogen fertilizers on a newly sodded lawn until it's mature. I suggest at least three months of established growth before using a nitrogen-rich fertilizer.

Make sure you select fresh sod rolls (*top*): look for a deep green colour, and stay away from sod that has brown or yellow patches. Before laying sod, put down a layer of good topsoil and then rake it until it's level with the existing lawn (*bottom*).

 **Early Spring** Lawn

When laying new sod, roll out the pieces in a brickwork pattern (*facing page*). Butt the joints together, making sure there are no gaps between the pieces (*above left*). Cut any excess with a sharp knife (*above right*), doing your best to avoid small pieces, which may dry out before taking root.

# Get Stretching

After a winter of sitting on the couch, your body likely isn't in the best condition for you to be dragging a rake around for an entire day. Always remember to stretch and make sure you take breaks between your early spring gardening tasks. If gardening is hard on your back, you may want to invest in a rake with an ergonomic handle. And don't forget to ask for a spousal back massage après gardening!

A bit of stretching can help your body avoid an injury. Start by bending forward to stretch your hamstrings (*top left*). Then, leaning on a spade for support, lunge forward to stretch out your legs (*top right*). Finally, put the spade behind your neck (*bottom left*) and gently rotate your torso, holding for a few seconds when you're fully extended (*bottom right*).

# Raking Thatch

**E**ven a healthy lawn loves a light raking in early spring to remove excess thatch. Thatch is the dead grass that blankets your lawn. A little bit of thatch is healthy, but anything over 1 cm (1/2 inch) can prevent moisture and nutrients from getting down where they're needed. It can also provide an excellent home for unwanted insects and a breeding ground for disease. Dethatching also helps increase airflow to areas matted by heavy snow and helps remove sand and salt from lawn areas close to roads, driveways, and walkways. Toss some of the excess thatch into the composter and put the rest out with the yard waste.

Use a fan rake—the same kind you use to rake leaves in the fall—and be gentle, so you don't damage the lawn as it's coming out of hibernation. If you have a big lawn, raking can be exhausting, so always do this work in small stints. For large areas, purchase a dethatching rake or rent a power rake. There are several types of power rake: some work like commercial-quality string trimmers, while others are push-behind tools that work like lawn mowers. Either way, power raking makes dethatching quick and easy, so speak with your neighbours about splitting a full-day rental fee with them.

You can leave about 1 cm (1/2 inch) of thatch (*left*) on your lawn, but anything more can impede the flow of moisture and nutrients to its roots. Dethatch using a rake with closely spaced metal tines (*right*) to remove excess material, and put it into in the composter.

# Repairing Damage

By the time you're done raking all that thatch, you may have discovered some damage that the snow was hiding for the last few months. So while you're waiting to get your hands dirty in the garden, at least you'll have something to keep you busy!

### Grubs

Does your lawn look like a motocross trail with burrows, divots, and torn strips of sod? This damage is caused by nocturnal creatures searching for a food they love: grubs. Grubs are the larvae of Japanese or June beetles, and they're an early-spring delicacy for skunks, raccoons, moles, and even some birds.

The best solution is to get rid of the grubs themselves, but early spring is not the time to do that: the grubs are typically deep underground at that point, so most control measures won't work then. (See page 204 in the Summer chapter for more on grub control.) To discourage skunks and raccoons from digging, I cover the affected areas with blood meal, as its odour should keep them away. Your neighbour may suggest using mothballs, but these are toxic, and if they're ingested by a dog, a cat, or a child, you're looking at a much greater problem than damage to your lawn.

Ugh, grubs. These beetle larvae can do a lot of damage to your lawn—and so can the raccoons and skunks that rip up the turf looking for them.

## Frankie's Tip

Moles can make your lawn look like a war zone, but I've found that anything that creates a vibration underground will deter them. My favourite gadgets are the inexpensive whirligigs that can be found at local garden centres and dollar stores. When the whirligig turns in the wind, it creates a vibration at its base that irritates burrowing moles. Seriously, this works!

7047
9.0327-74

GROWN IN CANADA
CULTIVÉ AU CANADA

### Dog spots

If your family got a puppy last Christmas, you may discover your lawn has small, well-defined burned patches all over it. These are urine spots, courtesy of your furry friend. Dog urine is full of lawn-damaging things like nitrates, tin, and ammonia, and the problem seems to be greater with female dogs. Repairing dog spots is a four-step process: rake to remove the dead grass, apply horticultural lime to neutralize the urine, top-dress with soil, and reseed. You can buy all-in-one products for dog spots, but in that case, you're just paying for convenience. (Your dog's diet can be at fault here, and there are meal supplements that can help. Training your dog to relieve herself in a specific location can also help. If you catch your dog in the act, quickly wash the area to dilute the urine.)

*Get Growing*

Man's best friend can be your lawn's worst enemy (*top left*)! To repair "dog spots" at any time of year, start by raking out as much of the dead grass as possible (*top right*). Put down a layer of topsoil and some horticultural lime to neutralize the acid (*bottom left*). Then sprinkle a layer of good-quality grass seed (*bottom centre*) and cover lightly with topsoil. As always with any new grass seed, make sure to water well (*bottom right*).

**Early Spring** Lawn

### Snow mould

If your lawn has areas that get a lot of piled-up snow, you may have to deal with snow mould, a fungal disease caused by compaction, lack of light, and moisture. It typically occurs in shady areas, where snow is very slow to melt. Snow mould can cause irregular brown patches and a greyish-pink, cottony fungus. It rarely kills grass, though, and the problem usually corrects itself as the ground dries out and the lawn starts to grow. To speed the recovery, I always suggest a light raking with a top-dress and light broadcast of seed. To help prevent snow mould, spread any heavy or drifted snow across the lawn to speed the melting process.

## Aerating Your Lawn

If you have clay-based soil or a high-traffic lawn—or if your grass has struggled over the last few years, you should aerate. When you aerate your lawn, you punch holes in the soil to loosen the compaction and allow water, nutrients, and oxygen to get down to your lawn's roots. If you have a small area, you can do this by repeatedly pressing a pitchfork a couple of inches into the turf and giving it a wiggle.

For larger areas, core aeration is the way to go. With this process, a gas-powered machine is used to extract plugs of soil from the lawn. You can rent a core aerator from a rental store and do it yourself (split the cost with your neighbours), but this is heavy work that might be best left to a lawn maintenance company. Early spring is an ideal time to aerate, but you have to wait until the lawn is no longer soggy.

## Thickening Your Lawn

If your lawn is undamaged but a little on the sparse side, you can thicken it up by top-dressing and overseeding. Top-dressing means covering the lawn with a thin layer of nutrient-rich material. The ideal time to do this is after you've aerated your lawn.

Here's my do-it-yourself recipe, which includes the seed and fertilizer too. You can mix the material like a salad in a wheelbarrow or on the driveway. The mix should cover about 70 square metres (750 square feet) of existing lawn. Allow one to three weeks for the seed to germinate:

* 120 litre (approx. 3.8 cubic ft. compressed) bag of loose peat moss
* 80 litre (3 cubic ft.) bag of vermiculite
* 1 kg (2.2 lb.) good-quality grass seed
* 5 kg (11 lb.) bag of seed-and-sod starter

Use a long-handled spade to spread the mixture over any area you want to thicken. Then use a fan rake to even it out. Make sure you don't smother the grass underneath: a layer of about half a centimetre (1/4 inch) should do it. Give your newly top-dressed lawn a good watering if there's no rain in the forecast.

I use an even lazier method to keep my grass thick. Every two weeks during spring and fall, I use my small hand broadcaster and spread grass seed across my lawn. I usually time this so the seeding is done just before a period of rain. Just be careful not to get too much grass seed into your garden! And you'll need to make sure that the seed stays damp for at least three to four days to encourage germination.

Quick trick: If you're aerating a small area of lawn, a simple pitchfork will do the trick. Just press the fork a couple of inches into the lawn and wiggle it back and forth (*left*). The holes you leave behind will allow air and water to get to the roots (*right*).

When top-dressing a lawn, you want to cover the existing grass lightly, being careful not to suffocate it.

To spread grass seed in a small area, you can broadcast it with a simple plastic container. For larger areas, use a handheld or walk-behind spreader.

# Where Lawns Won't Work

Sure, you want that perfect patch of grass, but there are places where lawns just don't work:

**Under large shade trees**
For these problem areas, I recommend removing the turf and using mulch (any kind will do—cedar, pine bark, and beach stone are all excellent choices) or creating a dry shade garden.

**Awkward, tight corners that are hard to mow**
I suggest removing sod and installing low-maintenance ground cover.

**Spaces between houses with little or no light**
Just use mulch—no plant will grow in darkness.

**High-traffic areas**
Constant foot traffic eventually scrapes away the sod and compacts the soil. Why not just install a walkway?

## Mowing

Most lawns remain dormant during early spring and generally require mowing only when warm temperatures are followed by rain. But trust me on this one: after raking and just before fertilizing, adjust your lawn mower to cut at 6 cm (2 1/2 inches) and give the grass a quick trim. This will clean up the outer edges that may have been burned by winter conditions, and many times, it will push your lawn into active growth.

Make sure your mower blade is sharp. If you have a good-quality blade, you can remove it with a socket wrench and take it to a rental store, hardware store, or small-engine repair shop for sharpening. (Or you may find it's cheaper to just buy a new blade.) Cutting your lawn with a dull blade can cause a lot of damage, like a bad haircut. Would you want your hair stylist to use dull scissors? I recommend using a mulching blade, which leaves the clippings on the lawn, where they break down quickly and provide nutrients.

## Fertilizing

Once spring flowers are popping out of the ground and birds are chirping, it's time to fertilize. Lawns truly are like hungry bears coming out of hibernation in early spring. But remember, plants need food only when they're actively growing. Fertilizing too early is wasteful and can be damaging to the environment.

The best way to make sure you have a healthy and lush lawn is to fertilize in early spring with a quality, slow-release fertilizer that's high in nitrogen, such as 27-0-0 or 29-2-4.

Not all fertilizers are created equal: manufacturers and retailers can be a little tricky. You may see one fertilizer selling for $9 per bag, while another bag of the same weight is more than double that price. But the $9 bag won't cover the same area because much of its weight could be made up of fillers. As a rule, the more lawn a fertilizer can cover, the better the quality (because higher-quality fertilizer

*Get Growing*

can be spread more thinly). It's worth paying a bit more for the good stuff. Ideally, choose a slow-release fertilizer, which prevents burning by introducing nutrients gradually, at a rate the plant can manage.

Read the label to see how much coverage your fertilizer will give, and adjust your fertilizer spreader accordingly. The bag will tell you how to set your spreader. If you're in doubt about how much to apply, err on the side of too little (too much can burn your lawn).

Note that organic lawn fertilizers usually cover a smaller area because they have less nitrogen. I would love to tell you that organic fertilizers work great, but the truth is they just don't have a high enough concentration to stimulate deep green growth.

# Fertilizer: The Numbers Game

Fertilizer is always identified with three numbers, known as the N-P-K ratio. The numbers indicate the percentage of nitrogen (N), phosphorus (P), and potassium (K) in the fertilizer mix. For example, an early spring lawn fertilizer might be labelled 29–2-4, which means it's 29 per cent nitrogen, 2 per cent phosphorus, and 4 per cent potassium. (The rest is filler or other nutrients.) Each of these nutrients plays a specific role in your lawn:

**Nitrogen** helps plants produce chlorophyll, which promotes new green growth. This nutrient is especially important for plants that are made up mostly of foliage. That includes grass, which is why you use a fertilizer such as 27–0-0 or 29–2-4 to green up your lawn in spring.

**Phosphorus** promotes strong root growth in lawns. You don't want to promote tender top growth in the fall because that growth would be damaged by the cold weather. That's why fall lawn fertilizers have less nitrogen and more phosphorus. They might be labelled 5–10-5, for instance.

**Potassium** contributes to the general health of a plant, guarding against disease and making it more tolerant of drought and cold. Fall fertilizers often contain 5 per cent to 18 per cent potassium, which helps protect against the ravages of winter.

# Weeding

It's time to make your peace with weeds. Yes, most of us want a lush, weed-free lawn, but let's be realistic. If you need to use toxic chemicals and strain our water resources to get it, then a perfect-looking lawn is really not perfect at all.

Some weeds can actually benefit your lawn. Take white clover, for example. This so-called weed remains green under the toughest conditions, feels great on bare feet, requires little or no mowing, and never needs fertilizing. In fact, clover is a "nitrogen-fixing legume," which means that it feeds itself. Many low-maintenance or eco-lawn mixes now combine clover with grass seed so the two can support each other.

Early spring is the only time to prevent crabgrass from growing. This particularly stubborn weed has wide, yellowish-green (sometimes reddish) blades that taper to a point. Crabgrass is an annual weed, which means it needs to reseed itself to survive: it produces finger-like purple seed heads when mature. Crabgrass typically invades poor or weak lawns, especially in sunny areas.

Crabgrass seeds won't usually germinate in early spring, as they need a soil temperature of 15°C (59°F), with daytime highs of 20°C (68°F) for several days. That gives you an opportunity to use a weed preventer, which coats seeds and stops them from germinating. (Unlike an herbicide, however, it does not kill existing weeds.) The most common weed preventer is

White clover

corn gluten, a granular product you apply with a spreader, like fertilizer. Unfortunately, it takes a lot of corn gluten to prevent crabgrass from growing: most suggest a rate of 10 kg (22 lb.) per 93 square metres (1,000 square feet) of lawn. You also need to plan ahead if you're going to use corn gluten because you cannot reseed your lawn for up to four months after applying a weed preventer. (Another downside is that birds and mice love to eat corn gluten: I once left a bag in my garage over the winter, only to find a fat mouse napping near it in spring!)

While a sprinkling of weeds in a lawn is fine, we all have our limits. I use the 50/50 rule here too: if your lawn is 50 per cent weeds, consider starting over. See above for instructions on creating a new lawn from scratch.

Corn gluten (*above*) won't kill existing weeds, but it will prevent weed seeds (especially crabgrass) from germinating. Just make sure to check the bag for directions so you don't over-apply.

*Get Growing*

# FLOWER GARDEN

**Your early-spring flower garden checklist:**

✔ Assess any winter damage and clean up the garden as necessary.

✔ Remove as many weeds as you can before they go to seed.

✔ Prune trees and shrubs to promote healthy growth.

✔ Plan, dig, and prepare your garden beds.

✔ Take special care when preparing a garden on a slope.

✔ Divide mature perennials and find a new home for them.

✔ Transplant shrubs and perennials as necessary.

✔ Add new perennials and shrubs, water thoroughly, and protect with mulch.

✔ Fertilize, but only after plants begin active growth.

✔ Add colour with cool-season annuals such as pansies.

## Sizing Up Your Property

Your first garden task in early spring is to inspect your property for winter damage. Take a few moments to walk around and see how the winter treated your plants. Prune any stems that may be broken due to heavy snow.

If trunks of small fruit trees have been chewed by hungry wildlife (rabbits, mice, deer), make a note to protect them—I'll tell you how in the Fall chapter. Evergreens may have turned brown from "winter burn" (moisture loss). Employ the 50/50 rule again: if the browning is over 50 per cent, remove the evergreen and start over.

A clean garden is a healthy garden. So after your inspection, remove any debris in the garden—including dead leaves, dead foliage, and dead stems from perennials (if you didn't cut these back last fall) and any annuals that are still kicking around from last season. If you piled mulch on any of your plants for winter protec-tion, uncover those plants now. Just be careful not to do this too early or you'll leave your plants vulnerable to cold nights.

As you walk around your property, make a list of the material you'll need to get your early spring jobs done—yard waste bags, maybe a new set of pruners. This will keep you and your budget under control. I've worked in a garden centre since I was a child, and our family has always banked on huge impulse sales in early spring. Eager gardeners just like you are so pumped up that they buy every pretty thing they see. Going to a garden centre in spring without a list is like going to a grocery store hungry!

A clean garden is a healthy garden! As soon as the forsythias are in bloom, it's time to clean leaves and other debris from garden beds (*left*). Cut away dead stems from your perennials to make room for new shoots that will emerge soon (*right*).

My essential tools for the garden: spade, trowel, rake, garden fork, pruners, garden knife, watering can, and a good pair of gloves.

*Get Growing*

# Weeding

I know you're anxious to get planting, but first things first. Many weeds go to seed in the spring, so pulling them out early will help your gardens stay weed-free later in the season. In the world of weeds, an hour today can save you a whole day in the weeks to come.

The best time to weed a garden is immediately after a gradual rain because at that time, the roots will be loose and easily removed. (For perennial weeds like dandelions, you must remove the entire root system or they will just grow back bigger.) If you've ever watched TV infomercials, you'll know that there's a tool for every weeding job imaginable. But you can get by with these essentials:

* a three-prong cultivator or a hoe (for small weeds with shallow roots)
* a dandelion digger that pulls out the weed by the root (I recommend the stand-up model from Fiskars)
* a weeding fork (a kitchen fork will do in a pinch)

A propane weeding torch can be great fun—just don't use it close to a wooden deck, wooden planter, or dried leaves!

As you do your early spring weeding, you may worry that you'll accidentally pull out a perennial plant that's just starting to push through the soil. It does take some experience to distinguish between garden plants and weeds at this time of

If you don't have a weeding fork, a regular kitchen fork will do (*left*). Just make sure it's good quality and doesn't bend easily. If you forgot to clean up your tools last fall, give them a good once-over with a wire brush to start the season right (*above*).

year, so I remember what my grandfather used to say about picking mushrooms: "Only pick what you know or you're going to be in trouble." I also recommend that you mark or tag new plants in fall to make early spring weeding easier.

When you remove weeds, avoid carrying them across your garden or lawn, as the seeds are easily dispersed: put them in a bag, bushel, or wheelbarrow. You can toss weeds into a composter, but I don't recommend it: place them at the curb alongside the rest of your garden waste instead. Municipal composting programs sterilize the soil, which kills weed seeds. Small home composters just don't heat up enough to do that, so if you put the weeds in your own composter, you'll end up putting the weed seeds back in your garden.

## Pruning

Pruning is a method of selectively cutting the branches of a tree or shrub to improve its appearance and performance. Plants are rarely harmed by pruning, and indeed, some need severe pruning in order to thrive. Plants such as butterfly bush will even benefit from being pruned right to the ground in early spring.

Trees and shrubs that flower or bear fruit on new wood need to be pruned now. ("New wood" is this year's growth.) This includes raspberries, most hydrangeas, and pretty much any shrub that flowers in late summer or fall. Lilacs, on the other hand, bloom on old wood or the previous year's growth. Pruning a lilac in early spring will remove the flower buds set late last season, so if you do that, you won't get flowers this year. As a no-fail rule, prune a lilac only after it blooms.

Start by removing any jagged areas from broken stems. For small shrubs and bushes, use handheld pruning shears. There are two basic types: bypass pruners, which have two blades that slide like scissors, and anvil pruners, which strike against each other like bolt cutters. Both designs work well, but make sure you buy a good-quality tool, which will likely cost upwards of $30. (Cheap pruners can damage your plants and may not even last a season.) Clean the blades after every use to prevent rust, and keep the blades sharp: you can buy a sharpener specifically designed for pruners.

Larger branches may require loppers or telescoping pole pruners, while heavy tree branches should be removed with a pruning saw or even a chainsaw. Don't be afraid to get the help of a professional service if you have a large or difficult job. Tree branches are a lot heavier than they look, and cutting them is dangerous. The higher the branch, the greater the risk.

Many people recommend coating freshly cut tree branches with pruning paste. Don't do it! Studies have shown that pruning paste provides no benefit and may slow the healing process.

Normally you should only prune one-third of a shrub, but butterfly bush is an exception. You can cut this vigorous grower back to half its size in early spring. Don't worry: it will look sparse when you're done, but it will grow back healthier than ever by mid-summer.

"Prune after bloom" is my rule of thumb, but you should prune any broken or diseased stems immediately. Keep your pruners sharp so they will make nice, clean cuts.

**Early Spring** Flower Garden

## Pruning Clematis

Clematis is beautiful, but the many varieties can keep you guessing about the right time to prune them. The first step is determining which of the three main types of clematis you have:

**Spring bloomers** flower on last year's growth, so you prune these guys after they bloom.

**Summer and fall bloomers** flower on this year's growth, so they need to be pruned now, in early spring, when they are just coming out of dormancy.

**Repeat bloomers** flower in spring and then again later in the season. With these varieties, I just remove any dead wood, pruning back in early spring to where buds are showing. Later in the season, just deadhead (cut off the dead flowers only) and thin them out to create some airflow.

Many clematis varieties can be pruned vigorously, but never remove more than one-third of overall growth at any one time.

# Preparing Your Garden Beds

**W**hether you're breaking ground for a new garden bed or renovating an existing one, preparation and planning are the keys to good results.

There's something so rewarding about tearing up the turf to create your own piece of Eden. But remember—and I will say this often—you need to be realistic. Before expanding a garden, ask yourself some questions: Do I have time to take care of it? What is the purpose of the garden? Does it add a benefit—aesthetic or practical—to my family or my property? Do I have the budget to expand?

### Outlining

Nothing completes the look of a garden bed like a nice, clean edge. During the early spring, take a sharp spade and tidy up the edges of your existing beds.

If you're expanding your garden, use your hose (or a combination of several hoses) to outline any new beds. Step back and visualize the space. Once you're happy with the shape, use a spade to cut along the inside edge of the hose or spray the edge with marking paint.

Should you use plastic edging? It does prevent grass from growing into the bed, but a clean edge created with a spade—and touched up a few times a season—does the same job and looks better. Also, as the garden grows, you may need to expand your bed, which means your edging will need to be removed. In my experience, edging just adds cost, and it's not worth it.

### Sod removal

Some gardeners favour tilling sod or turning it over, but I prefer to remove it altogether. Removing sod reduces the chances of grass growing through the garden later on. Unfortunately, removing sod with a spade or a manual sod cutter is hard work: for large areas, you can rent a gas-powered sod stripper.

You may have heard that you can clear a grassy area by solarization—by taking a large black tarp or plastic sheet and placing it over the area for several weeks or even months. The heat and the lack of light and air will kill any grass or weeds under the tarp. However, it's too cool to do this in early spring, and even in summer, it takes a long time and doesn't always work.

To spray small areas, you can use non-selective herbicides such as WipeOut® and WeedOut®. In some provinces, these herbicides have become costly, as only ready-to-use forms are available, and you pay for this convenience. Herbicides work best on a sunny, dry day. Never use a non-selective herbicide on a windy day. If you do, you may end up killing your garden plants.

> **Frankie's Tip**
>
> When preparing a new garden bed, always pay attention to where your outdoor taps are. The garden farthest from the tap gets taken care of the least. If your new garden bed is far from a tap, consider creating a water-wise garden with native plants.

Use your garden hose to trace the outline of your new garden bed (*top left*). Move the hose around until you're comfortable with your design. Then use a sharp spade to cut along the line (*top right*). When removing sod, slide your spade horizontally so you cut through the roots while removing as little soil as possible (*bottom left*). The finished edge (*bottom right*) not only looks clean and neat, it also prevents weeds from spreading from your lawn into your garden.

*Get Growing*

## Soil amendment

Nine out of ten properties I visit have lousy soil, particularly in new subdivisions. That means that when you're digging a new garden bed, you'll need to amend the soil. (See the explanation of soil structure in the Introduction.)

How much soil should you add? The more, the merrier! Although this can be costly, money spent on soil is an investment in a good garden. I recommend at least 20 cm (8 inches) of good organic matter, though the ideal amount for new gardens is 40 to 45 cm (16 to 18 inches). Buy your soil from someone you trust: I've seen clean fill sold as topsoil! Make sure the soil is screened and shredded: this process filters out rocks, sticks, and other things that lower the quality.

Rain or shine, it's soil amending time! Early spring is a great time to add a couple of bags of composted manure to your flower and vegetable gardens to enrich the soil. Don't get overly excited like I do here and throw the soil around—dig it in gently to avoid disturbing the roots.

 **Early Spring** Flower Garden

| Soil type | What it is | When to use it |
|---|---|---|
| Topsoil | The surface layer of soil, usually dark in colour and rich in nutrients and microorganisms. Bagged topsoil is sometimes referred to as garden soil, black earth, or "muck." | In gardens and lawns to improve absorption of water and add nutrients. Use topsoil to amend sandy soils and to top-dress or patch lawns. Don't use it in containers: it's slow to dry out and can cause root rot (use potting soil instead). |
| Triple mix (3-in-1 mix) | A combination of three main soil types: topsoil, peat moss, and compost (usually composted manure). | In gardens to add nutrients and amend poor soils and to top-dress lawns. Don't use it in containers (use potting soil instead). |
| Manure | Animal feces, primarily from sheep or cattle. The manure used in gardens is composted: it has been allowed to decompose over a long period, ensuring that it won't burn your plants. (That's also why it doesn't stink.) | In gardens to add nutrients to poor soils and improve plant performance. Manure is an excellent fertilizer in vegetable gardens, where it can increase yields. |
| Peat moss | Decayed plant matter (technically called "sphagnum") that is harvested from bogs. Peat moss is acidic and nutrient poor, but it absorbs moisture like a sponge. | To improve the water retention in sandy soils, to loosen clay, and to lower the pH in soil (giving a boost to acid-loving plants like rhododendrons). Peat moss is also the main ingredient in potting soil. |
| Sand | Fine particles of mineral and stone, containing little or no organic matter. | As an amendment to improve the drainage of compacted soils in lawns and gardens. Also used as a base for patios and walkways. |

| Soil type | What it is | When to use it |
| --- | --- | --- |
| Compost | Plant, animal, or fish material that has decayed over a long period of time. | To enrich nutrient-poor soil and improve the health of plants in flower and vegetable gardens. You can use it in containers as long as it's mixed with peat moss. |
| Potting soil | A combination of peat moss, perlite, sand, and sometimes vermiculite. Also called "container soil" or "soilless mix," it is lightweight and absorbs a lot of moisture, but it has no nutrients unless fertilizers are added. | In pots and containers indoors and out. Potting soil has the ability to hold water but also dries out quickly, ensuring that plants will not drown or suffer from root rot. (Some plants, such as cactus and orchids, may require specialized potting soils.) |

### Planning it out

Draw up your plan. On a sheet of paper, sketch your new garden beds or any changes you've made to existing spaces. (Your diagram doesn't have to be fancy, but you should draw it to scale.) Now plan where you would like to position trees, shrubs, and perennials.

Lay out your new plants. When you eventually bring your new shrubs and perennials home, place them—pots and all—in the garden according to your plan. Step back and size up the garden from several angles. Have you remembered to position taller plants in the back and smaller ones up front? Do you have too many plants crammed into the space? Move things around until you're satisfied.

## Gardening on a Slope

If you're planning to dig a new garden bed on a slope, you should know that an undertaking like this is not for the faint of heart! As soon as you remove sod or existing plants from a slope, you run the risk of erosion. A flash rainfall can make a big mess.

The steeper the slope, the greater the risk and, typically, the greater the cost to retain it. Slopes with sandy bases are the most difficult to

Periwinkle is a tough and durable choice for a shady slope.

retain because sand can easily wash away. My general rules: a grade of 3 per cent needs no special attention, while one between 3 per cent and 10 per cent will require some method of erosion control. You can use a method as simple as planting perennials or shrubs with aggressive root systems or placing some stones in strategic positions. Any slope greater than 10 per cent will need to be retained, and a slope of 20 per cent or more with a drop of more than 30 cm (12 inches) in height will need the assistance of a landscape professional.

You can control erosion using retaining walls built from pressure-treated lumber or stone. You can also use plants that have vigorous root systems, including periwinkle, bugleweed, stonecrop, spreading juniper, ornamental grasses, and lace shrub (most of the time I don't worry about latin names, but here it's helpful—*Stephanandra incisa* 'Crispa').

Erosion mats—which you may have seen retaining earth on highway embankments—are also available. They're made of straw, which is biodegradable, and they're designed to hold soil in place until plants establish themselves.

Stonecrop is a drought-tolerant choice for slopes with poor soil.

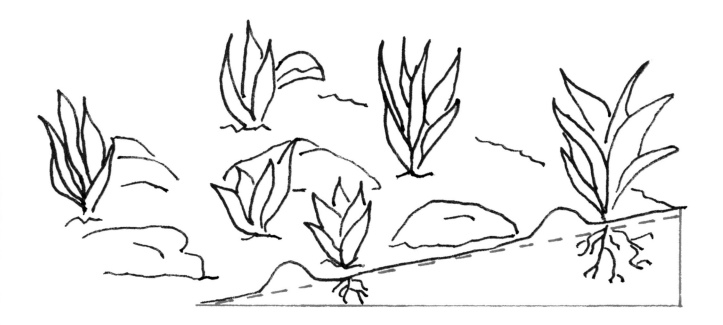

A slope of 10 per cent rises one metre for every 10 metres of horizontal ground. Slopes less steep than this require only simple erosion control, such as landscape rocks or mulch.

*Get Growing*

Steeper slopes require retaining walls. If you're building a garden with a slope greater than 20 per cent, get help from a landscaping professional.

## Design Disasters

When you design your garden, try to avoid these common pitfalls:

**Not paying attention to mature plant sizes.** Sure, it's nice to have a small evergreen by the entrance so you can put Christmas lights on it, but in 15 years you won't be able to get out the door! When selecting plants, read the tag or ask the garden centre staff about mature heights and spreads. This is where your graph paper to scale is a benefit: you can plot in your plants and enlarge them, showing where they will end up over time.

**Planting too close together.** This design disaster is related to the previous one. If your garden looks great immediately after planting, you've overplanted and overspent. In time, as plants grow to their mature sizes, you'll have a whole lot of tearing out to do. If you're worried that your garden will look sparse in the first couple of years, use annuals to fill the spaces between your young perennials and shrubs.

**Forgetting about the seasons.** Most communities in Canada experience four distinct seasons, so don't make the mistake of planting a garden that looks great only in spring or summer. Select a variety of plants that provide interest in each season: forsythia and tulips for early bloom in spring, day lilies for summer flowers, burning bush for vibrant red foliage in the fall, and evergreens to add colour in winter.

**Letting looks win out over function.** While you want your garden to look pretty, it shouldn't interfere with the way you use your property. Taking away part of your lawn to add an additional garden bed may not be the best choice if you have kids who love to kick a soccer ball.

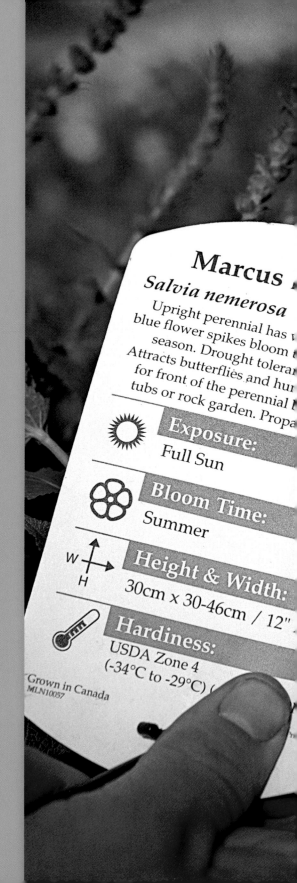

**Lack of balance.** Here I'm talking about too much patio and too little garden, too much wood and not enough stone, too many evergreens and not enough colour. A landscape is meant to look as natural as possible, and nature is all about contrast and balance.

**Poor use of space.** Small and large spaces can present challenges, but you can use them to your advantage. Small spaces can be made to feel larger through the use of colour and focal points that direct the eye. Larger spaces can feel more intimate if designed with bold colours.

**Poorly chosen colours.** Colour can both help and harm the impact of your garden. Bright shades of yellow and orange can overwhelm a small space, where calm pastels may be a better choice. In fact, soft pinks and purples can even make spaces appear larger. You should also pay attention to the time of day: an all-white garden at night will reflect the light and add drama to the space, but in the bright afternoon sun, the same garden will lack appeal.

**Buying plants because they were on sale.** Yes, it was a great deal, but does it fit your plan?

**Overthinking your garden.** The most difficult garden to design is your own, and sometimes the best solution is a fresh pair of eyes. Bounce ideas off friends and family. Take a picture of your property into a local garden centre and ask for suggestions.

Overplanting is a common and costly beginner's mistake. To ensure you don't place plants too close together, check the tag to learn each plant's mature height and width.

# Dividing Perennials

To the inexperienced gardener, it may seem like madness to dig up a healthy plant and chop it in two. But mature perennial gardens benefit from being divided. Like people, plants lose some of their vigour as they get older: you may notice that they have fewer blooms or weaker growth. Dividing older perennials stimulates new root growth, increases airflow, and gives the plant a new lease on life. It's also a great way to fill out your garden free of charge!

Early spring is the time to divide perennials that flower in late spring, summer, or fall. It's also the time to divide plants that have only foliage and no flowers. Plants that are easy to divide in early spring include hostas, day lilies, sedum, black-eyed Susan, and coneflower. I prefer to divide perennials as soon as their small eyes are popping out of the soil: that's when they're easiest to deal with. (The "eyes" I'm referring to are the first things that come out of the ground in spring. They'll later turn into green shoots, but at the "eye" stage, they're just round stubs of green growth.)

For dividing your perennials, choose a day that is cool and overcast, with rain forecasted in the near future. This weather is ideal, as it does not place your plants under stress. You'll need several tools: a sharp spade, a garden knife, pots, soil, and a hose or watering can. With your spade, dig around the perennial's roots and carefully lift out the plant. If the perennial is too big to come out in one piece, use your spade to cut the root ball in half or even in thirds: just place your spade between the eyes of new growth that have appeared at the surface of the soil. (The root ball is made up of all the roots lying below the cluster of plant eyes and all the soil that goes with them.) Then lift one section of the plant out of the ground and leave the rest in place.

If you've lifted out the entire plant, use your spade or garden knife to create a division. Look for any natural separations and use your knife to cut through the plant in those areas. The divided perennial should be immediately transplanted or placed with additional soil into a pot to give to friends or family. Your goal is to minimize shock to the roots, and keeping them moist is crucial. For short trips to neighbouring gardens, the divisions can be wrapped in moist newspaper. In areas where you've removed a division but left part of the plant behind, you'll need to immediately replace the soil around the remaining perennial.

# Transplanting Trees, Shrubs, and Perennials

I have to warn you: any time you transplant a tree, shrub, or perennial, you run the risk of losing it. The larger and older the plant, the greater the chance of killing it. So before you attack a well-established plant with your spade, make sure you have a good reason—maybe you mistakenly planted a tall plant in front of a shorter one, for example, or maybe you need to dig out some of the garden to expand your deck.

Early spring is an ideal time to transplant: cool temperatures and frequent rain will give the plant plenty of time to take root in its new location before stressful summer conditions set

in. Heat and drought kill plants more often than even the most frigid winter weather.

When transplanting, try to disturb the roots as little as possible. As when you're dividing perennials, a cool overcast day with forecasted rain is ideal. Never transplant during a period of drought, and never transplant during the hottest part of the day. Doing so is not just hard on your plants, but on you as well.

When you're transplanting, it's best to immediately put the plant in its new location—which means preparing the hole beforehand. My rule of thumb is to dig a hole twice the width and one-and-a-half times the depth of the root ball. Use your spade to measure for appropriate depth. Add a layer of good soil at the base of the hole (for clay or compacted areas, use a layer of coarse stone for drainage), and then lightly water the hole.

When the hole is ready, dig around the tree or shrub to a diameter that matches the farthest extension of the branches. (This is called

You can transplant peonies as soon as the "eyes" (the purplish spiky bits you can see in the photo above) emerge from the soil. Dig under and around the plant with a spade and gently lift it out of the ground (*top left*). Plant your peonies in the new location so the eyes are just visible. If you plant them too deep, they won't bloom!

Dividing perennials in early spring is easy, since you don't have to contend with a lot of top growth. Use a garden fork or spade to dig around the plant (*top left*). Then lift out the plant gently and look for a natural division in the root ball (*top right*). Sometimes, like here, the plant will naturally divide. If it doesn't, use a spade to remove a portion of the plant (*bottom left*) and place the division in your newly dug hole (*bottom right*) or wrap it in newspaper and share with a friend (*facing page*)!

*Get Growing*

Before planting a tree or shrub, use your spade to make a rough measurement, then dig a hole about twice the width and one-and-a-half times the depth of the root ball. Mulch your new plant heavily to retain moisture. Water it deeply with a slowly dripping hose or a watering bag.

*Get Growing*

the "drip line.") Dig down and around until you've formed a root ball. Your goal is to keep this root ball intact. For small trees and shrubs, this is easily done by wrapping landscape fabric around the ball to secure the soil. For larger trees, I suggest using a tarp: tuck it under the root ball and then use the tarp to lift the tree—with some helpers. (You may have to bribe some friends with beer for this job: work first, drink later.) You should consider hiring a professional when moving trees with trunks over 6 cm (2 1/2 inches) in diameter and more than 3.5 metres (12 feet) tall.

Place the root ball in the new hole so its top is about 1 cm (1/2 inch) above the ground. Then firmly backfill with good garden soil, using your foot to pack it down. If it's a tree you've planted, you may need to stake it to make sure it has all the support it needs while it's setting down roots. Finish with a transplant fertilizer. Deeper, less frequent (rather than constant, shallower) watering combined with regular applications of transplant fertilizer will help to minimize shock and ensure a healthy transplant. Deep watering is needed so that roots go way down into the soil rather than staying closer to the surface to get their water. To make sure the water goes deep, soak the soil slowly over a long period of time. Using a soaker hose is a good way of doing this. Be a soaker, not a sprinkler.

# Adding New Plants

When you add new trees, shrubs, and perennials in early spring, make sure you're planting locally grown stock that has been acclimatized to your area. Many garden centres in Canada bring in plants from warmer regions outside your province, often from the United States. If these trees or shrubs have tender growth and you have a flash freeze, that new growth will get burned off.

If you've recently added a few inches of new soil to your garden bed, give it some time to settle before planting trees or shrubs—this could take a few days or even a week. I have sometimes planted immediately following a garden prep, but after the new soil settles, the tops of the root balls become exposed. So I end up having to replant them. (This doesn't harm the plants, but it's a nuisance.)

## Planting

Before you dig your hole, water your plants thoroughly while they're still in the containers: planting them dry will put them under stress and reduce their chances of success. Then dig a hole double the width and one-and-a-half times the depth of the container. Put a layer of good soil at the base of the hole (add some stone for drainage if you have clay) and pour in a little water.

Now remove the container by carefully turning it upside down while you have a firm grip on the base of the plant. Loosen the root

## Frankie's Tip

The instructions for planting a new tree or shrub are almost identical to those for replanting a transplanted one. The only difference? You'll be removing your tree or shrub from the container it was in when it came from the nursery, so to minimize the shock, water it fully before you start, and then take care in removing it from its original container. (You may want to use your garden knife to cut away the container.)

The first step when planting new perennials is removing any junk—bricks, rocks, old beer cans—from the area (*top left*). Loosen the root ball with your fingers (*top right*) or with a sharp knife and place it in the hole. Add some rich topsoil and pack it down (*bottom left*). Keep the plant tag so you can refer back to it later: leave it in the ground (*bottom right*), or store it in an envelope indoors.

*Get Growing*

ball by going around the inside edge of the container with a knife or spade. Then place the plant into the hole, ensuring that the top of the root ball is just slightly above ground level (the plant will settle). Backfill with good garden soil and firmly pack the soil down to remove air pockets. Create a slight reservoir around the base of the plant and water deeply. A friendly reminder: deep watering is done by watering slowly over a long period of time, so that the water soaks far down into the soil, encouraging nice, strong roots.

Fertilize immediately with a water-soluble transplant fertilizer. If you're planting a large shade tree or evergreen, I recommend staking it, especially if it's in a windy area.

## Watering

Newly planted gardens need more frequent watering. Your plants probably received daily watering at the nursery or garden centre, and you need to wean them away from that slowly. Frequent watering also establishes strong roots and helps new plants adapt to their surroundings. I know I keep saying this, but water your new garden deeply to train plant roots to dive deep into the soil. Shallow watering encourages plants to send their roots close to the surface, where they can easily get dried out and damaged. A soaker hose is great for watering slowly and deeply.

With a newly planted tree, I often recommend placing your hose at the base, turning on the tap to a slow trickle and leaving it there for several hours—until the water has deeply penetrated the soil. (Never do this if the tree is near your home's foundation because you'll

Water new plants heavily but infrequently to train their roots to go deep into the soil.

Newly planted trees should be watered slowly and deeply. One of the best ways to do this is with a watering bag, which releases water gradually into the tree's roots.

**Early Spring** Flower Garden

Before planting a shrub, water it deeply while it's still in the container to reduce stress on the roots (*top left*). Use a spade to measure the size of the hole (*top right*): it should be double the width and one-and-a-half times the depth of the container. Remove the container without disturbing the roots, place the shrub in the hole (*bottom left*), and water deeply (*bottom right*).

Why bother with expensive and awkward landscape fabric when you can use newspaper instead? Lay a couple of sheets over the soil (*top left*) and cover with a couple of inches of mulch (*top right*). If you want to plant in that area later, just push the mulch aside (*bottom left*), cut the newspaper with a knife, and add your new plant. When you're done, give the mulch a light rake to keep it looking neat (*bottom right*).

**Early Spring** Flower Garden

then risk flooding your basement!) You can also buy "watering bags" that attach to the base of a new tree and slowly release water into the soil. After this initial soaking, keep watering the tree by letting the hose drip slowly at its base for 15 minutes at a time, twice a week.

### Mulching

Adding 3 to 8 cm (1 to 3 inches) of mulch is the only way to reduce weeding, protect plant roots, reduce erosion, and retain moisture in a garden. Some suggest using landscape fabric to bring the same benefits, but I disagree. It's time consuming to put in place and it gets in the way every time you want to add new plants. I prefer just to use old newspapers: place them on the soil four or five sheets thick and then put the mulch on top. The newspaper will allow water to soak through and will break down over time.

## Fertilizing Your Plants

For the first two months, newly planted gardens should be fertilized only with a transplant fertilizer that focuses on the development of roots and not on upper growth or blooms. A plant that is firmly rooted in the first season will perform for many years to come. Transplant fertilizers typically have higher middle numbers (phosphorus), such as 10-52-10. You'll find the proper application rate on the label.

Established plants will benefit from a general-purpose fertilizer in early spring once they're actively growing. Look for new green growth that signals the plants are waking up from winter. Fertilizer comes in many forms, suited to many different uses in the garden.

Here are some guidelines to help you decide which ones to choose:

* Water-soluble fertilizers come in powdered form and need to be mixed and diluted in water. (Miracle-Gro is a popular example.) These are a bit labour intensive, but they work well on both annual and perennial flowers.

* Liquid fertilizers are also good general-purpose products. They may be premixed, but they generally come in a concentrated form and need to be mixed and diluted in water.

* Granular or pellet fertilizer is best applied using a handheld spreader or shaker. This fertilizer is similar to the stuff you use on your lawn: there are even slow-release types designed to fertilize the garden over an entire growing season. This isn't as effective as feeding with a water-soluble product, but if you're strapped for time, it's better than nothing.

* Fertilizer spikes, which are inserted into the soil around a tree or shrub, are an even lazier way of fertilizing and are very inconsistent. I'm not a fan of them.

* Organic fertilizers include compost teas, fish emulsion, coffee grounds, and potato water (the water left in the pot after you boil potatoes). Soil amendments such as compost, peat moss, and manure, as well as bone meal and blood meal, are other examples of organic fertilizers.

In all cases, the best time to fertilize is after a rain or after you've watered the garden. Watering opens up the soil and the roots, so the plants will take up the nutrients easily.

Fertilizer comes in a wide array of forms. All purpose 20-20-20 fertilizer is water soluble and sure to give you a "blue thumb" (*top left*). Liquid fertilizer needs to be diluted in a watering can (*top right*). Lawn fertilizer comes in small pellets (*bottom left*) that are broadcast using a spreader. Fertilizer spikes (*bottom right*) can be used to feed tree and shrub roots, but I'm not a fan of them.

## The Magic Numbers

Earlier in this chapter, I explained that the three numbers on lawn fertilizer labels indicate the percentage of nitrogen, phosphorus, and potassium. You'll notice the same "N-P-K" numbers on garden fertilizers.

### Nitrogen

Nitrogen-heavy fertilizers (like 30-12-12) promote lush, green top growth.

### Phosphorus

Phosphorous feeds the roots and leads to big blooms. Transplant fertilizers (such as 10-52-10) are high in phosphorus to jumpstart the roots of new plants.

### Potassium

Potassium promotes the overall health of plants, strengthening them against disease and harsh weather. Fertilizers high in both phosphorus and potassium will also promote blooms and are a good choice for ornamental flowers.

Fertilizers vary widely, so always make sure to read the label to understand what the product is intended for and how it should be applied.

## Choosing Annuals for Early Spring

On one of those beautiful April afternoons when the temperature hits 20°C (68°F), you may be tempted to start planting annuals in your garden. You need to resist that temptation! It's common for the thermometer to dip below freezing overnight in early spring, and frost is fatal to tender annual plants.

One of the first rules of successful gardening is to avoid planting non-hardy annuals until all danger of frost has passed. This list includes impatiens, petunias, begonias, coleus, and many other annuals you see stacked in trays at the garden centre. Purchasing and planting these too early in the garden season is a waste of money.

If you are dying to see some colour in early spring, you do have some frost-tolerant choices. Cool-season annuals will usually survive a run-in with Jack Frost, although flowers, buds, and leaves can be damaged and may need time to rebound.

Pansies are symbols of early spring. You can plant them as soon as the soil is workable in the garden. Plant them in mass groupings in the most visible parts of your garden for the biggest colour impact. The fragrant flowers are even edible: if you want to make a fancy dish, place them in a salad for a little floral decoration. Pansies perform well in spring, but the extreme heat of summer puts them and other frost-tolerant annuals into a state of dormancy. They become leggy and unattractive, and they may need to be replaced with summer annuals such as geraniums or wax begonias.

## Other cool-season annuals

viola

snapdragon

osteospermum

dianthus

stock

dusty miller

# Growing from Seed

Don't get too caught up in the seed aisle at garden centres in early spring. While you may be enticed to purchase trays, starter soil, and seeds of your favourite plants, be aware that growing plants from seed takes a lot of time and space. Ask yourself if it's worth it. Marigolds, for example, are easy to grow from seed. But you need to weigh the effort of preparing the trays, nurturing their growth, taking them outdoors to harden off before planting, and trying your best to prevent damping off (a fungus that can kill overwatered seedlings). Why go through all that—especially if you're new to gardening—when you can buy a tray of healthy marigolds for $10?

Direct sowing is the process of planting seeds right in the garden as opposed to starting them in pots. Early spring gives you the opportunity to direct-sow a whole host of annuals, including my favourite: sweet pea (above). Look at the seed package to see when direct sowing is recommended. A tip for my fellow lovers of sweet pea: before planting, soak the seeds for 12 to 24 hours. For hard-shelled seeds, soaking increases germination success and speeds up the growing process.

You can add colour in the early spring garden with some frost-tolerant annuals (*top left*). Two of my favourite varieties are pansies (*top right*). and osteospermum (*bottom right*). When planting, loosen the root ball by giving it a squeeze (*bottom left*), and then pack down the soil around the base of the plant. Pinching off the blooms will send more energy to the plant's roots and improve performance later in the season.

*Get Growing*

# VEGETABLE GARDEN

**Your early-spring vegetable garden checklist:**

✔ Choose an appropriate site for your first vegetable garden.

✔ Remove the sod and amend the soil with composted manure.

✔ Select vegetables that you and your family enjoy eating.

✔ Plan your garden so taller plants won't shade out smaller ones.

✔ Plant cool-season vegetables, such as radishes and lettuce.

✔ Plan ahead to add summer vegetables (such as tomatoes) when early crops are done.

✔ Plant asparagus or rhubarb, two perennial vegetables.

✔ Plant raspberries and strawberries.

✔ Consider adding a fruit tree to your property.

**E**arly spring is the ideal time to prepare a vegetable garden. Growing your own vegetables has many rewards, but it takes a lot more effort than hitting the produce section at the grocery store. If you're a novice, don't let your stomach do the planning because it's your back that will end up doing the work!

Many people are too ambitious when they plant a vegetable garden. The bigger the garden, the more weeding, watering, and harvesting you'll be doing. Even a small vegetable garden can provide a bounty: by harvesting, replanting, and rotating your plants, a space as small as 1.5 square metres (16 square feet) can feed one person for an entire season. One zucchini plant can make a lot of zucchini loaf, and a single tomato plant grown under the right conditions will produce enough tomatoes to keep a family of four happy.

## Digging a New Vegetable Garden

**A** successful vegetable garden requires an area with at least six hours of direct sunlight per day, so start by choosing a good location on your property. Soil is king: a garden built on rich, fertile soil with good drainage will result in great yields even without much fertilization. Choose a site close to a direct water source.

After you have selected the site and determined the size of your new garden, the next task is the most difficult: removing the sod. See my suggestions in the Flower Garden section, above.

Old-time gardeners will tell you to "double dig" a new vegetable garden. This is a lot of work (you'll be ready for that massage when you're done), but it's well worth it, especially if you're preparing a small area. The benefit of double digging is that it improves the subsoil, which in many residential areas is clay, sand, or worse.

Start by digging out an area to a depth of 20 cm (8 inches) and put the soil into a wheelbarrow or off to the side. Use a garden fork to break up the compacted subsoil, making a trench along one side of the area you are digging out. Then dig out a trench next to that first trench and turn the soil from the first trench into the second one. Keep breaking up the subsoil in that way (putting the subsoil from one trench into the previous trench) until you've completed the entire garden area. Then backfill the last trench with the soil you set aside in the wheelbarrow or off to the side.

If this all sounds like too much work, I've got another suggestion for new vegetable gardens: build boxes with 2" x 10" or 2" x 12" lumber. Raised boxes warm up more quickly in the spring, offer good drainage, and best of all, they allow you to build on top of hard, clay soil. Here's a tip: don't use pressure-treated lumber, which contains chemicals that may leach into the soil. To prevent the wood from rotting, I like to line the insides of the boxes with landscape fabric or I use a water sealer—like the one you'd use on your deck. Boxes can be a great way to get kids involved in gardening—not only are they at kid height, but you can grow something and then eat it!

Whether you double dig or build raised beds, it's essential to use rich, organic soil in vegetable gardens. For best results, use a soil that includes composted manure, such as triple mix.

Removing sod for a new garden bed (*facing page top*): hard work, but someone's got to do it! Double digging will tax your muscles, but the results are worth it. Divide the area into several trenches, then remove the surface soil from one trench (*facing page bottom*) and place it in a wheelbarrow. Loosen the subsoil, and then start digging the second trench (*top*). Put the surface soil from the second trench into the first (*bottom*) and repeat the process. After digging the last trench, back-fill it with the soil you set aside in the wheelbarrow.

A raised bed is the best way to grow vegetables in an area with poor soil. Fill the raised bed with good topsoil (*facing page*) and add a generous helping of composted manure, then level it with a rake (*above*). Before planting, I like to use the handle of the rake to mark properly spaced rows (*left*).

# Planning Your Crops

**E**arly spring is the ideal time to map out your vegetable garden and decide what you want to plant. Never run to a garden centre and just grab the vegetable plants that look cool or the ones with pretty pictures—they may not be suited to your location. And don't plant what you won't eat!

Write down the types of veggies you want to grow. Next, on a sheet of graph paper, draw out the dimensions of your garden. Now let the plotting begin. Pay attention to how wide and tall the plants will grow—the mature height and spacing will be on the tag. A farmer once taught me to always plant vegetables in rows running north-south, with tall vegetables on the east side, so they don't shade out the smaller ones. If it makes more sense to plant rows east-west in your garden, plant the tallest veggies on the north side. Be sure to leave some space so you can move between the plants.

Your vegetable garden will constantly evolve during the season and over the years. As soon as the ground is no longer spongy when walked on, you can start sowing "cool crops" such as broad beans, beets, endives, carrots, leeks, lettuce, onions, parsnips, peas, potatoes, radishes, spinach, Swiss chard, and turnips. These plants can take a bit of frost, and they may be ready to harvest just four to six weeks after you sow the seeds: radishes and most leafy green vegetables are early favourites. Save some seed—and some space—if you want to plant a second crop later.

Other vegetables can't be planted until later in the spring, and they may take a long time to start producing. You can maximize the productivity of your vegetable garden by using a technique called "succession planting." For example, after harvesting your radishes and lettuce, you can plant tender crops such as tomatoes or corn in the same soil.

Try to rotate your crops occasionally: don't grow your broccoli or tomatoes in the same place year after year. If you do, you run the risk of spreading overwintering diseases. Planting the same plants in the same place also means you'll be using up the same nutrients in the soil. Planting a different crop will ensure healthy plants and great yields.

If you fell into the trap of purchasing and planting your tomatoes too early, you can still protect them from frost. If you planted them in pots, just bring them indoors at night. Otherwise, try building a simple frame around the plants and covering them with a frost blanket, bedsheet, or towel. (Avoid using plastic sheets: if a plant touches the plastic, the frost can still form.) Smaller plants can

## Frankie's Tip

A friend—let's call him Steve—once bragged to me that he had a direct source to a farm and all the free manure he could haul. Well, this manure was fresh—still steaming, actually—and instead of fertilizing his plants, it killed them. Fresh manure is highly acidic, so it will burn your plants. Manure needs to be rotted or composted for months before it can be used in the garden. Don't worry, any manure you buy at the garden centre is composted: that's why it doesn't smell. Just don't be like Steve and think you can put fresh animal waste on your plants.

2047
9.0327-74

GROWN IN CANADA
CULTIVÉ AU CANADA

5
PP

be covered with newspaper or a plastic pot overnight.

Watering your garden thoroughly the night before—or scheduling sprinklers to water your garden before sunrise—can also work: water droplets give off heat as they evaporate, and with temperatures hovering just around freezing, this may be enough to keep frost at bay.

Here's a trivia question for you: what vegetable crops don't need to be planted every year? In most of Canada, there are actually only two: asparagus and rhubarb. Early spring is a good time to purchase and plant these perennials as long as the risk of severe frost has passed.

You can plant "cool crops" such as Swiss chard, radishes, and lettuce from seed as soon as the ground is no longer spongy. Space the seeds carefully according to the directions on the package.

**Early Spring** Vegetable Garden

Asparagus is the first harvest of the spring season! This vegetable takes time to become established: the roots require deep planting to 75 cm (30 inches), and you should not expect a harvest until the second or third year. The good news is that a weed-free, well-planted asparagus bed can provide a bounty of produce for up to 30 years.

If you have a shady spot in the vegetable garden, rhubarb may be your friend: it can grow well with a minimum of four hours of sunlight. Its large leaves and thick stalks add interest to the garden. The key to success is adding well-rotted manure in spring and fall. (Note that while rhubarb stalks make great pies, the leaves of this plant are toxic. I don't even like to throw them in the compost—I put them in my yard waste.)

### Frankie's Tip

You'll often read that a vegetable should be planted a certain number of days after your "last frost date." This refers to the date when overnight temperatures in your area have historically always been above freezing, which means that the threat of frost has passed. (You can find last frost dates in your region at www.almanac.com.) Frost is always a danger in early spring, especially in low-lying areas.

Crops that start peeking out of the ground early: chives (*left*) and rhubarb (*right*)

# Raspberries and Strawberries

**W**ith the early spring comes your opportunity to plant berries, which also come back every year. Plant raspberries in full sun in well-drained soil. Summer-bearing raspberries (which produce in late spring) bear fruit on last year's growth, so don't prune the canes in early spring—then you'd be saying goodbye to your harvest! Ever-bearing raspberries (which produce all summer) bear fruit on this year's growth, so cut them to 5 cm (2 inches) above the ground in early spring. A word of warning: raspberries spread easily, so consider planting these in a contained, raised bed.

If you want to grow strawberries, you have a couple of options. Summer-bearing varieties give you one crop of berries in June, while the ever-bearing plants produce a June crop, take a rest, and then produce more berries on a lesser scale until frost. I recommend that beginning gardeners stick to the ever-bearing varieties, which are easier to maintain.

Strawberry plants love full sun, but they'll also do fine in partial sun as long as the soil is

rich and well drained. They need a fair bit of room, so space them 30 cm (12 inches) apart and leave at least 90 cm (36 inches) between rows. Strawberry roots like to lie near the surface, so dig a shallow hole, water it, and place the plant in the hole, spreading the roots out horizontally. Take extra care not to bury the crown, as this could cause the plant to rot. (The crown is the section of the plant between the bottom stem and the roots.) Water deeply after planting, and be sure to keep this part of the garden well watered: since the roots are close to the surface, they can dry out quickly. Mulch the strawberry plants with clean straw or leaves to maintain moisture.

## Growing Fruit Trees

**H**ave you ever dreamed of picking an apple or plucking a pear right from your own backyard? If so, you might want to purchase and plant fruit trees—and early spring is the time to do that.

Apples, pears, and plums are the hardiest fruit trees and therefore the best for overwintering in Canada, but all fruit trees require full sun. Almost all varieties currently sold are semi-dwarf, which are much more manageable than full-size fruit trees. While some are self-pollinating, other fruit trees require a compatible tree within the same area if you want to be sure to get fruit. Self-pollinators include most cherry trees and some varieties of plum (look on the tag or ask the nursery staff).

Word of warning: fruit trees can attract wasps and can also be some work; they need annual pruning (in late winter or very early spring), frequent inspection for insects and disease, and spraying during the growing season. When pruning a fruit tree, you're looking to maximize airflow by removing any inward growing branches and any stems that are rubbing against each other. Diseased, broken, and dead stems should be removed throughout the year.

**By now, your garden will be looking fresh, clean, and ready for the warmer weeks of spring. Sit tight until Jack Frost disappears for another season. Then it's time for spring planting!**

Spring

# Let the Planting Begin

I think Robin Williams said it best: "Spring is nature's way of saying, 'Let's party!'" The trees are just about fully foliated, the grass is growing (weeds are too!), tulips, daffodils, and magnolias dazzle you with their colours, and the fragrance of lilacs and apple blossoms is in the air. Everything is taking on the green hues that mark a new year in the garden.

Early spring was all about preparation: raking, repairing, digging, and weeding. Mid- to late spring is when all that hard work gives way to fun. There's nothing quite like the feeling of standing in your yard with a dozen containers of colourful new plants and a freshly dug garden stretched out in front of you. So many possibilities!

Spring is also when you start to feel the pressure of keeping up with the neighbours by planting a garden that will outperform the one you planted last year. The garden centres know this, and it makes them see dollar signs. Beware: like the dessert table to dieters, your garden centre is full of temptation. If you visit without a plan, you'll leave with a full vehicle and an empty wallet. Before you head out to do your shopping, make those lists again!

# FLOWER GARDEN

### Your spring flower garden checklist:

✔ Deadhead tulips, daffodils, and other bulbs that have finished flowering.

✔ Plant summer-flowering bulbs such as gladioli and dahlias.

✔ Select, purchase, and plant new perennials.

✔ Address problem areas—such as those with too much shade or poor soil—by selecting specific perennials for these conditions.

✔ Choose low-maintenance rose varieties.

✔ Fertilize, prune, and stake your perennials as necessary.

✔ Consider planting showy biennials such as hollyhocks and foxgloves.

✔ Add instant colour to your garden with annuals.

✔ Plant containers using my "thrill, fill, spill" recipe.

✔ Prune trees and shrubs that have finished flowering.

✔ Look for caterpillar infestation in trees and take steps to remove the insects.

Spring in the flower garden is a busy time! Deadheading, planting, pruning, and weeding will keep you hopping. Once again, take a deep breath. They didn't build Rome in a day, and you won't built a great garden in one season—but with a little TLC, you'll see some amazing changes. Just tackle one job at a time and enjoy the results.

# Dealing with Spring-Flowering Bulbs

**T**ulips, daffodils, and crocuses are beautiful in bloom, but afterwards they look pretty ugly. However, tempting as it may be, don't rip out that untidy foliage: it serves an important purpose. The leaves of all bulbs should be left as long as possible, as they provide food for the next year's blooms. Crocuses do fine if they are cut back a little earlier, but the same isn't true for hyacinths, daffodils, and tulips. Leave these until they become brown. That can take a few weeks, but you'll have so many spring jobs in the garden that you won't get bored waiting!

As the flower heads wither and dry on the plant, they need to be deadheaded. Deadheading is simply using your pruning shears to cut off the stems that hold spent flowers. (Get used to this: it's what you'll be doing during all your spare time until October!) If you don't deadhead, the withered flowers will draw out energy that you would rather have go to next year's blooms.

# Planting Summer-Flowering Bulbs

**M**ost people think of bulbs as something you plant in the fall for spring blooms. But many summer-flowering plants grow from tender bulbs, corms, tubers, or rhizomes that are planted in spring because they will not overwinter.

Many people call all of these underground storage devices "bulbs," and we'll do the same

I had to cut back these tulips to make room for another plant, but I try not to remove the foliage until the leaves are fully brown.

in this section to keep things simple. But you can impress your gardening friends by learning the differences:

* If you split open a bulb, you'll notice that it has several layers, like an onion. The inside of the bulb contains a complete miniature version of the plant—you can think of it as an embryo. Tulips and daffodils are the most common flowers that come from bulbs.
* Corms often look like bulbs on the outside, but they don't have layers: they are actually just the base of the plant's stem. Crocus and gladiolus both grow from corms.
* A tuber is also a stem structure, though unlike a corm, it doesn't have a protective covering. Most tubers are vegetables—the potato is the one people are most familiar with—but dahlias are also an example of a tuber.
* Rhizomes are root systems that spread horizontally and look like gnarled wood or ginger root. Irises and Canna lilies grow from rhizomes.

Summer-flowering bulbs are easy to grow and provide a jolt of vibrant colour in the garden. The only downside is that they must be removed from the garden in fall and stored indoors in a cool, dry spot during the winter, and then re-planted next spring. The real trick is finding them in the garden after a long season! I recommend using green plant markers (available at garden centres), which you stick in the ground on top of the bulbs. In a pinch, you can even use Popsicle sticks or pieces of old mini-blinds.

When purchasing your bulbs, remember that the bigger the bulb, the bigger the bloom (and the bigger the price tag). Never purchase bulbs that feel soft, look withered, or smell mouldy. If the bulb is already sprouting leaves, it could mean it was exposed to light and moisture. This could result in a weakened plant.

Wait until the danger of frost has passed before you plant summer-flowering bulbs. Dig a hole about three times the height of the bulb (check the package to make sure), add a little slow-release fertilizer such as Smart-cote or Osmocote, mix it into the soil, and place the bulb on top. Fill in your hole and water well.

Here are my favourite tender bulbs to plant in spring. Most require full sun and well-drained soil, although begonias and caladium perform well in partial shade.

### Caladium

Known as "elephant ears" for its broad leaves, caladium provides beautiful, colourful foliage for the shady part of your garden and gives a tropical look to planters. Caladium requires a long growing period, so you may want to purchase it as a small plant, rather than planting the corms yourself.

## Frankie's Tip

Planning to add more bulbs next fall and worried you won't remember where you need to add them? Buy a package of coloured Popsicle sticks from the dollar store and stick them in the ground where your bulbs are now (yellow for daffodils, red for tulips, purple for hyacinths, etc.). Then, when you're ready to plant in the fall, you'll know where to dig and where not to dig.

2047
9.0327-74

GROWN IN CANADA
CULTIVÉ AU CANADA

PP

Bulbs, such as these tulips, have layers like an onion.

Corms look like bulbs, but they don't have the same layered structure on the inside.

A tuber is a stem structure with no protective covering.

Rhizomes look like gnarled wood or ginger root.

**Spring** Flower Garden

### Canna lily

Like caladiums, Cannas require a long growing period and are best purchased in a pot. Nothing comes close to the tropical look of the Canna lily in a planter or a garden bed. It blooms in a variety of beautiful reds, oranges, and salmon, with outstanding leaf colour (some varieties have burgundy foliage). Fertilize and water them well, especially on hot summer days.

### Dahlia

Dahlias come in many different forms, colours, and sizes—from 15 cm (6 inches) tall to over a metre (3 feet) in height and from tiny, tight blooms to huge, shaggy flowers. If you plant them in full sun and water them often, you'll have lots of late-summer colour (as long as you remember to deadhead them). Dahlias are quite long lived—many gardeners dig and store their dahlia tubers for years.

### Gladiolus

A great, old-fashioned cut flower that can grow to a metre (3 feet) or more in height. Plant the corm in the back of the garden in full sun, and stake the stems to prevent them from bending and falling over. Gladiolus blooms in about two months, and if you plant the corms in two-week intervals as soon as the danger of frost has passed, you can enjoy a succession of blooms all season.

### Tuberous begonia

These shade-tolerant plants—not to be confused with wax begonias, which are popular annuals—come in trailing, compact, and bushy types. They reward you with colour throughout the summer in shades of red, pink, orange, and white. Double, rose-like blooms open above large-toothed leaves. They look great alongside impatiens.

## Choosing Healthy Plants

Garden centres are overflowing with stock in the spring. While you may find the selection overwhelming, take the time to carefully examine any plant you're planning to buy. Here's what to look for:

### Plants free of insects and disease

Check both the top and the underside of foliage for chew marks, discoloration, insects, mould, or browning.

### Buds, not blooms

With flowering plants, you're looking not for what is here, but what is yet to come. Don't immediately choose plants that are already blooming: instead look for plenty of unopened buds.

### Strong roots

When the garden centre staff is looking the other way, carefully remove the plant from the pot. The roots should be white and firm—if they look black and appear soft or rotten, stay away. If roots are growing out of the pot, that's also a bad sign: it may indicate an older plant that will have difficulty growing out of its potted form.

*Get Growing*

My favourite bulbs to plant in spring *clockwise from top left*: caladium, Canna lily, gladiolus, tuberous begonia, dahlia

Get the best value for your money at the garden centre. When you're picking out bulbs (*facing page*), give them a sniff to check for any odour of mould. A healthy bulb has no smell and is firm to the touch. Choose plants with vibrant green foliage (*top left*) and scan for signs of insect damage. The roots should be healthy and white (*top right*), never black, slimy, or growing through the bottom of the pot. Take a pass on weak plants with spent flowers like the one on the left (*bottom*) and select the healthiest and sturdiest available.

**Spring** Flower Garden

### Broken pots

Stay away from plants with broken pots or containers. This may be a sign that the plant was dropped, and the root system may be damaged.

### Short and stocky stems

Tall and leggy plants are usually unhealthy. Look for compact plants with strong stems.

### Vibrancy

This is hard to describe, but eventually you'll develop a feel for recognizing it. Healthy plants just ooze their willingness to grow. Look to the leaves: vibrant foliage is full and lush, with deep colour.

# Planting Perennials

A perennial is a plant that lives more than two years. (Annuals live for one year and biennials for two—more about those later.) Technically, trees and shrubs are perennials, too, but when gardeners use this term, they're usually talking about herbaceous plants—that is, those without woody stems.

The variety in a garden centre can be overwhelming! Remember to focus on plants that suit your garden in terms of sunlight, soil type, and mature size.

*Get Growing*

Although they are more expensive than annuals, perennials are a better long-term investment because they come back every year bigger and better. They usually require very little care after initial planting—other than fertilization once in the spring and a thorough watering once a week or so. Some perennials require deadheading to improve the plant's health, and some (such as delphiniums and peonies) need to be staked. Every few years, they need to be divided.

If you haven't divided or transplanted your perennials already, you can still do so throughout the spring. Wait for a day that is cool and overcast and make sure that the divisions are watered well for the first few weeks.

When choosing perennials for your garden, first determine the type of soil and the amount of light available, then consider the size of plant you need for the space. (Pay special attention to the plant's mature size: a common mistake that new gardeners make is planting tall plants at the front of a border.) The plant's tag should include all of this information.

If you're creating a new garden and need a lot of plants, why not have a perennial party? Invite friends over for a celebration of food, friendship, and fun, and ask each guest to bring a perennial from their garden. You'll wind up with a great garden at low cost, and the collection of plants will always remind you of your friends.

The chart on the next pages lists my favourite easy-to-grow perennials. All are perfect for the beginning gardener, as they do well in sun or partial shade and in any decent soil. None of them requires any special care, and success is (almost!) guaranteed. Note that some of the early-flowering varieties will be past their bloom time, so they won't flower in your garden until next year.

# Perennials for Problem Areas

Anyone can grow a garden in full sun and rich soil. But in the real world, every garden has problem areas. Some parts are shaded by trees, fences, or buildings, while other garden beds may have poor soil that you're not able to amend. Another common problem area is the far side of the yard that isn't easily accessible to the hose. Here are my suggestions for perennials to fill those troublesome spots.

## Frankie's Favourite Perennials for Shade

### Astilbe

This plant produces tall stems with feathery flowers in various shades of pink, red, and white. Astilbe performs well in partial to full shade but requires moist soil, as it likes to "keep its feet wet."

# Easy-to-Grow Perennials

| What it is | What it looks like | When it blooms | How tall it gets | What it needs | Why I love it |
|---|---|---|---|---|---|
| Candytuft | | April | 10–25 cm (4–10 inches) | Sun | Good for edging, rock gardens |
| Columbine | | May | 30–75 cm (12–30 inches) | Sun to partial shade | Cut flower, great in rock gardens |
| Bleeding heart | | May | 25–30 cm (10–12 inches) | Partial shade | Classic fave |
| Iris | | May | 30–60 cm (12–24 inches) | Sun | Spreading rhizomes are easy to divide |
| Peony | | June | 45–120 cm (18–48 inches) | Sun | Fragrant cut flower |
| Dianthus | | June | 10–45 cm (4–18 inches) | Sun | Many varieties |
| Lupine | | June | 60–120 cm (24–48 inches) | Sun to partial shade | Striking display |

| What it is | What it looks like | When it blooms | How tall it gets | What it needs | Why I love it |
|---|---|---|---|---|---|
| Day lily | | June | 30–90 cm (12–36 inches) | Sun to partial sun | New blooms daily |
| Astilbe | | July | 30–120 cm (12–48 inches) | Partial shade | Feathery blooms |
| Delphinium | | July | 150 cm (60 inches) | Sun | Cut flower |
| Shasta daisy | | July | 100 cm (39 inches) | Sun | Cheerful cut flower |
| Purple coneflower | | August | 60–150 cm (24–60 inches) | Sun to partial sun | Attracts butterflies, birds |
| Black-eyed Susan | | August | 60–90 cm (24–36 inches) | Sun to partial sun | Late bloomer |
| Sedum | | August | 30 cm (12 inches) | Sun to partial shade | Drought tolerant |

### Bleeding heart

Bleeding heart does well in shade or partial shade and requires moist, sandy soil. It has a distinctive, heart-shaped flower in pink or white, which hangs down from the stems. Some varieties will bloom throughout the summer. Bleeding heart grows from creeping rhizomes, although some varieties are "neater" and won't spread. About a month after blooming, prune the plant back heavily: you can reduce its size by about half.

### Coral bells

If you're looking to have some fun with foliage in the shady garden, consider coral bells. With leaves ranging from green to chartreuse, deep purple, and orange rust, this plant adds all-season interest, even though its flowers are usually inconspicuous.

### Ferns

Ferns are ideal for use in a perennial garden or a woodland setting. They grow in partial to full shade and provide a cool, romantic look. There are a huge number of varieties, but I suggest ostrich fern (*Matteuccia struthiopteris*) and Christmas fern (*Polystichum acrostichoides*). Pay attention to whether the fern can grow in dry shade or whether it needs "wet feet." Ferns can take a few years to become established, so don't be discouraged if they struggle at first.

### Hosta

I can't say enough about these plants: there is such a wide variety available that once you're turned on to them you can become an obsessed collector. Although used mostly for their beautiful foliage—which ranges from lime green to bluish grey, yellow, and white—hosta flowers can be elegant too. I love the white blooms and huge bluish leaves of 'Elegans' and the pale lavender flowers and yellowish folia of 'Albopicta'. Hostas can take full shade and do not require any special care. Slugs are always a danger with hostas, but some varieties are resistant, including 'Elegans', 'Zounds', and 'Blue Mammoth'.

### Virginia bluebells

This plant, native to Canada, grows to almost 60 cm (24 inches) and produces beautiful, bright blue flowers in spring. It does well in shade or partial shade and moist sandy soil.

## Frankie's Favourite Perennials for Poor Soil

### Alyssum

The 'Mountain Gold' variety of this sun-loving ground cover produces fragrant, bright yellow flowers and silver foliage at the front of a garden.

### Columbine

Flowering in spring, columbine comes in a wide variety of colours and heights. It thrives well in most soil types and in sun and partial shade. It will also recede easily.

### Day lily

Day lilies grow well in almost any conditions. In summer they produce new blooms every day in a wide range of colours. There are thousands of varieties, but my personal favourite is the 'Stella d'Oro'. It blooms continuously in brilliant yellow and has a more compact and controllable habit.

My favourite perennials for shade (*clockwise from top left*): astilbe, fern, hosta, Virginia bluebells, coral bells, and bleeding heart

 **Spring** Flower Garden

My favourite perennials for poor soil (*clockwise from top left*): alyssum, columbine, day lily, basil, lamium, and periwinkle

*Get Growing*

### Herbs

Many herbs thrive in poor conditions. Perennial herbs such as thyme, mint, oregano, and lavender thrive in infertile soil.

### Lamium

This ground cover does well in sun or shade. Plant it in the front of the garden and enjoy tiny flowers in shades of pink, purple, and white on foliage in all shades of green and green-white blends.

### Periwinkle

Another ground cover that thrives in shade (even under trees), periwinkle produces violet-blue spring flowers on deep green foliage.

## Frankie's Favourite Perennials for Dry Areas

### Coneflower

This drought-tolerant perennial has large, daisy-like flowers on 60 cm (24 inch) stems, blooming in late summer. 'Rubenstein' has purple flowers with a brown centre, while 'White Swan' has a yellow centre surrounded by white petals. 'Magnus' needs full sun and grows up to 1.5 metres (5 feet) tall.

### Coreopsis

Airy foliage and daisy-like flowers make these a midsummer favourite. There are many varieties between 30 and 60 cm (12 and 24 inches) tall. Plant them in full sun.

### Ornamental grasses

With many gardeners becoming more water conscious, ornamental grasses have become increasingly popular as accent plants. One variety, blue fescue, produces silvery, blue-green foliage and grows 10 to 25 cm (4 to 10 inches). Plant them in full sun.

### Sedum

Known for their durability and thick, succulent leaves, the many varieties of sedum range from low spreaders to tall compact forms. Low-growing varieties have foliage in blue-green, grey-green, red-green, or bronze-red, with tiny pink, yellow, or red blooms. The taller 'Autumn Joy' combines well with fall-flowering perennials: its attractive grey-green foliage produces light pink blooms darkening to burgundy on 24 to 60 cm (9 1/2 to 24 inch) stems in late fall.

### Thyme

Growing to 10 cm (4 inches) high, thyme is great as a ground cover or in the rock garden. It thrives in dry, infertile soil. Blooms are purple-pink or pure pink in late spring and early summer. Varieties include mother-of-thyme and 'Bressingham'.

## Frankie's Tip

The staff at your garden centre can often help you choose plants for problem areas. But if you're looking for personal attention, go during off times: early in the morning or early in the evening but never on the weekend. Garden centres are also packed when the sun is shining and the temperature goes up. The slowest times in the garden centre are rainy and cool days.

2047
9.0327-74

GROWN IN CANADA
CULTIVÉ AU CANADA

My favourite perennials for dry areas (*clockwise from top left*): coneflower, coreopsis, blue fescue, thyme, sedum

*Get Growing*

# Getting Started with Roses

Everyone loves the look and fragrance of roses, but I warn novice gardeners about them. Classic hybrid tea roses are beautiful, but they're waning in popularity because they can be pretty high maintenance and difficult to overwinter. Tree roses—the ones that have been grafted onto a tall stem—are also very difficult to overwinter. If you want to really challenge yourself as a gardener, go for it. But I would stay away from these if it's your first spring at the garden centre. My suggestions for newbies are the Canadian Explorer series (which were developed specifically for our climate), David Austin roses (old-fashioned English varieties), and Flower Carpet roses (low-growing varieties with massive blooms).

If you already have roses in your garden, you should prune them in spring to promote vigorous growth. Cut away any stems that are definitely dead (they'll be grey and brittle), as well as any very small or criss-crossing canes.

You can fertilize your established roses in spring, but newer bushes should be fertilized only after their first bloom. Use a fertilizer specially formulated for roses: it's available in granular or water-soluble form. Food for roses has a higher middle number (phosphorus). You can also use organic fertilizer or compost. Purchase enough to fertilize now, again in June, and finally in the middle of July.

Roses like to be watered well once a week—or more in very hot weather. Just remember two very important things when watering roses. First, always water the base of the plant and not the leaves. And second, always water in the morning and never at night. If rose leaves get too much moisture, the plant can develop a fungal disease called "blackspot."

## Frankie's Tip

*Plants in my garden live by the rule of two strikes. If I select a perennial, tree, shrub, or annual and it doesn't work even though I ensured it had the right light, water, soil type, and hardiness, I give it another chance. But if that plant fails to grow a second time, I say it's out. Time to determine a better selection for that spot in the garden!*

2047
9.0327-74

GROWN IN CANADA
CULTIVÉ AU CANADA

# Frankie's Must-Haves in Plant Selection

To earn a place in my garden, a plant must have at least three of the following qualities:

- multiple-season interest (such as unique stems, evergreen)
- a long bloom period
- unique or interesting foliage
- drought-tolerant
- disease or insect-resistant
- easy to grow, with minimal pruning and fertilizing
- doesn't need staking
- a proven track record (I've seen it work in gardens in my area)

When pruning roses, start by removing canes that are thinner than a pencil (*facing page*). Using sharp pruners, cut unwanted canes right back to a main stem (*above*).

**Spring** Flower Garden

# Plants You May Not Know Are Poisonous

If you have children or pets who like to visit your garden, it's best to avoid these plants:

**Bleeding heart.** Both the foliage and the roots are harmful if consumed in large quantities.

**Daphne.** The berries can be fatal, especially to young children.

**Elderberry.** The entire plant is poisonous (apart from the berries), but the roots are especially toxic.

**Oleander.** The stems, branches, and leaves are extremely dangerous if ingested.

**Rhubarb.** The stems are tasty but the leaves are extremely toxic—I don't even recommend putting them in the composter.

*Clockwise from top left:* bleeding heart, daphne, elderberry, oleander, rhubarb

# Helping Your Perennials Thrive

**M**ost perennials don't need a lot of maintenance, but there are a few things you can do in spring to help your flower garden thrive.

Fertilizing once a season is often enough, but supplementing with water-soluble fertilizer throughout the growing season can be helpful if your soil is nutrient poor.

Mums, asters, and garden phlox benefit from being pinched back in late spring or early summer. Trimming the new growth will encourage stockier stems and a more compact growth, with larger blooms in late summer or fall.

Some spring-flowering shrubs, such as 'Goldflame' spirea, will reward you with a second bloom when pruned after the initial flowering. You can cut back these vigorous growers pretty aggressively: prune them down by at least a third—or even more.

Forget-me-nots and bachelor's buttons (cornflower) become mouldy if left in the garden and can spread disease. They should be cut back by about half at the end of their bloom time.

Spring is the time to provide additional support to the stems of top-heavy plants. Before plants such as delphinium, hollyhock, and foxglove get too large and begin to bend, place a stake beside the stem and loosely tie with raffia, yarn, or covered wire (something that will not cut the stem). Continue tying along the stem as the plant grows.

Prune back forget-me-nots after these beautiful blooms are done.

 **Spring** Flower Garden

Now is also the time to put peony rings in place, before the plants get too big. These wire supports will keep the flower heads from hanging into the wet soil after a rain and make the whole garden looking neater. I like to use tomato cages for this purpose—although they are not as attractive, they are much cheaper and the plant soon covers them anyway.

Bushy plants such as shasta daisy, black-eyed Susan, and baby's breath can also get pretty sloppy later in the season. You can place stakes around the plants and run string around to hold them up.

You can purchase stakes at your garden centre in bamboo, wood, and wire, but I like to use tall, slim branches if possible. They blend in well and look natural.

## Planting Biennials

As you may have guessed from its name, a biennial plant lives for two years. Biennials do not produce flowers in their first season: they bloom only in their second year and then die. Some, like hollyhocks, reseed themselves and may come back year after year, while others need to be replaced every two years.

Get your peony rings in place while the plant's shoots are still small.

*Get Growing*

# My Favourite Biennials

| What it is | What it looks like | When it blooms | How tall it gets | What it needs | Why I love it |
|---|---|---|---|---|---|
| English daisy | | April–July | 15 cm (6 inches) | Full sun | Bright colours, early bloomer |
| Canterbury bells | | May–June | 60–90 cm (24–36 inches) | Partial shade | English country garden look |
| Hollyhock | | June | 180 cm (72 inches) | Sun to partial shade | Reseeds well, many colours |
| Foxglove | | June | 90–180 cm (36–72 inches) | Partial shade | Reseeds, many colours |

## Planting Annuals

If perennials are the fireworks, annuals are the fire. Whereas many perennials have short-lived explosions, annuals provide a constant flame of colour in the garden all season long.

Annuals live for just one growing season and must be purchased and planted every year. Many require frequent deadheading, fertilization, and watering to keep them vibrant throughout the summer season.

Remember when I warned you about getting out on the lawn too soon in spring? Same goes for planting annuals. Just because you're enjoying a spring weekend in shorts and sandals, it doesn't mean all danger of overnight frost has passed. You'll probably see flats of impatiens and petunias at grocery stores that look tempting, but remember: retailers aren't necessarily great gardeners.

Do not head to the garden centre without a plan! You will be overwhelmed by the varieties and colours available. Take some time to stroll around your property with a notebook and make some notes. Do you want to fill a bed with annuals only, perhaps in blocks of colour or at varying heights? Perhaps you want to plant annuals en masse around shrubs or evergreens. Think about mixing them in your perennial beds to provide pops of colour throughout the season. As you make your shopping list, consider your light requirements, proximity to a source of water, height, and colour.

Don't get stuck on one type of plant or on one specific colour. I like to work with one major colour theme for the garden, but be flexible enough to alter your theme based on what looks good at the garden centre.

Read the tags and make sure you follow the instructions about spacing. Many newly planted annual gardens look sparse for a few weeks until the plants become established. If you plant your flowers too close together, you won't harm them, but you'll have spent too much money!

When planting your annuals, follow these basic steps:

1. Water the plants while they're still in the containers.

2. Remove the flowers: this allows the plants to focus on growing roots.

3. Gently grip the plant at the base of the stem, squeeze the container, and carefully slide the plant out.

4. Loosen the root ball so it's no longer tightly bound in the shape of the container.

5. Dig a small hole for the plant and mix in a little topsoil or compost.

6. Place the plant in the hole and pat down the soil around it so the plant is firmly anchored.

7. Water deeply.

8. Fertilize.

Annuals perform best in well-drained soil that's rich in organic matter. Most also require full sun and regular watering. However, some annuals will thrive in different conditions.

## Frankie's Favourite Annuals for Partial Shade

### Ageratum
Commonly used as an edge at the front of the garden, ageratum has a compact or upright form with fluffy flowers in blue, white, and pink.

### Fuchsia
Available in feminine shades of pink and purple, these look best in hanging baskets.

### Lobelia
Available in shades of blue, pink, and white, lobelia varieties include compact upright forms (about 10–15 cm, or 4–6 inches), which make good edging, and spreading forms, which are ideal for hanging baskets and planters.

### Nasturtium
The edible flowers of this plant (available in hanging or upright forms) grow in bright shades of orange and yellow. Nasturtiums offer another advantage: they do well in poor soil.

Before planting annuals, water the plants thoroughly while they're still in the container. Turn the container upside down and gently slide the plant out (*middle left*), then loosen the roots by giving them a squeeze (*middle right*). Dig a small hole with your trowel and place the annual in the hole. Pat the soil firmly to remove any air pockets (*bottom left*). Pinching off the blooms (*bottom right*) allows the plant to focus on root development.

 **Spring** Flower Garden

### Nemesia

The dainty, fragrant flowers on this upright plant look great in planters and window boxes. It is a vigorous grower that loves hot, humid weather.

### Nicotiana

Red, white, pink, and even light green flowers bloom on this leafy plant, which grows to a height of 30 to 90 cm (12 to 36 inches). Some varieties are fragrant.

### Snapdragon

Who doesn't remember squeezing snapdragons to make their jaws open? This annual favourite is available in a wide range of colours—yellows, reds, pinks, and purples—or combinations of those colours. They're upright plants that grow to various heights.

### Sweet alyssum

With its tiny, fragrant flowers in white, pink, or purple, this makes an ideal edging plant. Your grandmother loved it—a proven performer that you should welcome to your garden.

### Thunbergia

Also called "black-eyed Susan vine," this plant comes in shades of yellow and white with dark centres. Useful for hanging baskets and large planters.

### Torenia

These are available in compact or trailing forms. They're similar to snapdragons and are available in pink, blue, or white.

Some of my partial shade favourites: ageratum (*above*), fuschia (*facing page, top*), lobelia (*facing page, bottom*)

 **Spring** Flower Garden

More great annuals for partial shade: Nasturtium (*top*), nemesia (*bottom left*), nicotiana (*bottom right*)

*Get Growing*

Snapdragons (*left*), sweet alyssum (*right*)

 **Spring** Flower Garden

Great annuals for shade: thunbergia (*left*), coleus (*right*)

*Get Growing*

## Frankie's Favourite Annuals for Shade

### Browallia

This upright plant grows 20 to 25 cm (8 to 10 inches) high and blooms with five-petalled, purplish blue flowers.

### Coleus

It doesn't bloom, but coleus has beautiful foliage—in shades of green, white, and red—that makes a unique addition to gardens, planters, and hanging baskets. Some varieties need partial sun.

### Impatiens

These are the most popular annuals for shade because of their constant blooms in bright hues of red, pink, orange, and white. Impatiens are available in different heights and in either trailing or upright form.

### Tuberous begonia

These begonias are sold as tubers in early spring, but later in the season, you'll typically find them as bedding plants in 4 inch pots. They have bright, rose-like, showy flowers in shades of pink, orange, red, and white. They thrive in shade but need lots of fertilizer.

### Wax begonia

This bedding plant's pink, white, or red flowers bloom on foliage with green and bronze tones. The short, upright plants (up to 30 cm, or 12 inches) look dramatic when mass-planted.

Browallia (*top*), torenia (*bottom*)

Impatiens (*top*), tuberous begonia (*bottom left*), wax begonia (*bottom right*)

**White** is excellent in shade and perfect near a deck or other part of the garden that you'll see at night. But in full sun, it's the worst choice, as the brightness of the daylight will wash your white away.

**Bright and bold oranges, yellows, and reds** are good choices for large properties because they jump out and make a space look and feel smaller. In a small space, bright and bold can feel anxious and uninviting.

**Pinks, purples, and cool blues** are calming selections that make small spaces intimate and may even make the space feel larger. But on large properties, soft and pastel colours can be lost in the landscape.

## Planting Containers

**N**othing is more welcoming than a container full of annuals by the front door, nothing more pleasing than bright plants on the deck on a Sunday morning, and nothing more handy than a selection of herbs by the kitchen door.

Many types of containers are available—terracotta, concrete, metal, fibreglass, wood, and resin—and it can be hard to decide which kind to use. Start by considering the exterior of your home: a square, steel planter will look great in front of a modern home, while a wood container will complement a home with a more rustic look. If your urn will be exposed to wind, you may want the extra weight of concrete or metal to hold it down.

Cost is always a factor, of course, and more expensive containers are typically more durable. But the most expensive is not always the best choice. For example, a lightweight resin or fibreglass container has the benefit of being easily moved: you can fill it with pansies and place it by the front door in spring, move it to the back and plant it with petunias in summer, and then bring it out front to display mums in the fall.

Ceramic and terracotta pots require more maintenance, as they need to be emptied and protected in winter. Bring them indoors, or at least turn them over so they won't fill with water that will freeze, expand, and crack the pot. Plantings in terracotta will also dry out faster, as these pots are more porous than others.

Any container can become a planter: before heading to the store, look around your home and use your imagination. Garage sales are great places to find items to use as planters, such as old wooden crates, baskets, buckets, and barrels. The only requirement is drainage: drill holes in the bottom of the container and add a layer of gravel or broken pottery.

You will need to buy potting soil for your containers, as regular garden soil is far too heavy. Potting soil has peat moss, perlite, sand, and sometimes vermiculite mixed into it, which makes the soil less dense. When soil is less dense it can retain moisture without becoming soggy. Potting mixes often come with slow-release fertilizer added. Check the label. Be sure to purchase

Choose a container style that suits the exterior of your home. Varieties include clay (*top left*), concrete (*top middle*), ceramic (*top right*), fibreglass (*bottom left*), and metal (*bottom right*).

I'm ready to plant a container with a Canna lily and some ornamental grasses. Stuff on my list: potting soil, broken bricks for drainage, time-release fertilizer, hand tools, and my trusty gardening gloves.

**Spring** Flower Garden

more than you think you need: it is amazing how much a pot will hold, and there is nothing worse than having to run back for more soil! Any extra will keep for another year.

I have a simple recipe for planting great containers—thrill, fill, and spill:

* The "thrill" comes from plants that give your container a "yak factor." (That is, your containers will be the talk of the town.) You'll want a plant with showy blooms, striking foliage, or dramatic height. My favourites include amaranthus (love-lies-bleeding), Canna, salvia (tall varieties), ornamental grasses, dracaena (spikes), and tropical hibiscus. You can also add interest to your containers with branches (curly willow, dogwood, birch) or obelisks (pyramidal supports), which can be used to grow vines.

* Adding "fill" refers to selecting plants of various heights so the entire container is covered: taller plants toward the centre, the shortest ones at the outside of the container, and plants in the middle gradually getting shorter from the centre to the outside. You can use foliage or flowering plants or a combination of both. Just try to avoid plants that will grow too tall or gangly. Buy them in odd numbers—three, five, or seven—and space them evenly around the circumference of your pot. I like to use petunias, geraniums, impatiens, begonias, and coleus.

* Around the very outside of the container, include a selection of plants that "spill" over the edge. Again, buy in odd numbers and plant evenly around the rim. I suggest ivy, vinca vine, verbena, alyssum, or 'Wave' petunias.

*Get Growing*

Place coarse gravel, plastic bottles, or broken bricks (*facing page top*) in the bottom of the container to improve drainage. Then add a potting mix (*facing page bottom*), leaving some room at the top. Add the tallest plant first (*above left*) and then fill the container with the smaller plants (*above right*). You can create a dramatic display with just two plant varieties, as long as there's good contrast in colour and form (*left*).

At the garden centre, arrange the plants together on your cart in the way they will be planted. Select colours that you enjoy, but don't overdo it. My rule of thumb is to have no more than three colours in any container. Sometimes selecting a few different plant types of the same colour can make for an interesting design.

You don't have to limit your container plants to annuals. Tropical plants, vegetables, edible flowers, perennial plants, and herbs can be used in containers—by themselves or in combination with other plants. (Perennials won't overwinter in a container, but in the fall, you can take them out of the container and plant them in the garden.)

Grouping containers together at staggered heights is another interesting display technique. Fill each container full of a single variety: use some pots for the thrill, others for the fill, and still others for the spill. Using an odd number of containers grouped together lets each plant variety show itself off. But be sure the containers themselves relate to each other in some way. If you make sure they're made of the same material or are the same colour or are similar in style, you'll have a display that's sure to please.

When you plant your containers, start with the tallest varieties and work from back to front or from the centre to the edges, depending on the shape and placement of the container. (If the container will be a "centrepiece," work from the centre to the edges. If it will be placed against a wall or fence, work from back to front.) For a 25 cm (10 inch) container, you'll likely have room for only 4 plants, while a 40 cm (16 inch) container will hold 7 to 10 plants.

## Caring for Trees and Shrubs

As you enjoy the beautiful spring blossoms in your neighbourhood, you may decide to add some flowering trees or shrubs to your own landscape. Fruit trees, flowering crab, dogwood, chestnut, and magnolia are some of the showy specimens that flower in spring.

You can continue to plant (or transplant) trees and shrubs throughout the spring. Garden centres offer lots of specials to entice you, but always make sure you have a suitable location. Trees are big and expensive, so if they won't fit, don't buy them! Make sure the trees and shrubs you buy are free of disease and insects, both of which can start to show up in the garden centre as the weather warms.

Follow the planting instructions in the Early Spring chapter, taking care to water sufficiently. In addition to an initial soaking that should last several hours, newly planted trees need a deep watering twice a week, which you can accomplish by letting a hose drip slowly at the base of the tree for about 15 minutes. Mature trees don't typically need watering, but if they look as if they're struggling, you can give them an hour's soak once a week if Mother Nature hasn't provided enough rain.

After planting, place mulch around the base of your new trees and shrubs. This not only looks good and keeps weeds away, but it will protect the tree from getting gouged by your lawn mower or trimmer.

## Pruning

Remember Frankie's rule: "Prune after bloom." All spring-flowering shrubs should be pruned after they've finished flowering. This will keep things looking tidy throughout the summer and gives the plant a full season to set new buds. Some shrubs, like spirea, may even give you a second bloom later in the season. Flowering almond, forsythia, and lilac are examples of spring-flowering shrubs that should be pruned after their spring bloom.

Shrubs that bloom on new wood (this year's growth) should also be pruned now if they were not cut back after they bloomed last year. These include late-summer- or fall-flowering plants such as false spirea and rose of Sharon. Prune these shrubs lightly by trimming off the tips of the branches (called "heading back") to decrease the size slightly and encourage bloom.

Here are some other tips to keep in mind as you patrol the spring garden with your pruning shears:

* Minimize plant stress by pruning on cool, overcast days.
* Keep your blades sharp and clean. When you're done for the day, sterilize the blades by wiping them with bleach to avoid spreading disease and then wipe them again with a bit of vegetable oil to keep them lubricated.
* Dead, damaged, or diseased branches should be removed to improve the overall health of the plant. Any branches that cross and touch, as well as those growing toward the centre of the tree, should also be removed. Make a clean, angled cut just above the visible bark "collar" near the trunk—the place where that branch connects to the larger branch or trunk. Make sure you don't cut into that main branch or trunk—you can hurt the tree that way.
* Severe pruning will rejuvenate older shrubs by stimulating stronger growth. Cut them back by about a third, pruning from the bottom to the top, ensuring that the widest part of the shrub is at the base so the plant gets plenty of light.

* Some bushes, such as lilac, send out suckers under the ground. Try to prune these off at soil level to prevent light from encouraging their growth. Otherwise, the bush will gradually take over your garden space!

* Keep pine and spruce dense by pruning off the growing tips (called "candles") each spring as soon as they've emerged from their papery sheaths. A light pruning any time until mid-August will keep evergreen shrubs such as cedar, cypress, and juniper to their original size and shape.

Large, mature trees need to be pruned to be kept healthy and looking neat. I strongly advise seeking the help of a professional arborist for this job: pruning large branches can be dangerous to you, to surrounding buildings, and to the tree itself. This can be expensive, but it needs to done only every three or four years in spring.

### Fertilizing

For flowering or fruit-bearing shrubs and trees, a fertilizer rich in phosphorus (a higher middle number) needs to be applied in spring. You can use granular or water-soluble fertilizer: apply it to all the soil inside the drip line (the maximum extension of the leaves) in order to reach all the roots.

Evergreen trees and shrubs, on the other hand, require nitrogen (a higher first number) just as your lawn does. These fertilizers can be applied in early spring to early summer, using the same drip-line method.

When you remove dead branches or side shoots from a tree, butt them right back to the trunk (*left*). In the same way, dead stems of a shrub can be cut right at soil level (*right*).

# Keeping Caterpillars at Bay

**Y**ou and your family aren't the only ones who enjoy spending time in the spring garden: several species of insects also think gardens are wonderful places to live. The most potentially harmful are hungry caterpillars.

Tent caterpillars are those squirming things you find hanging off the branches of trees, encased in a thick, tent-shaped web. They're commonly found on fruit trees, flowering trees, or bushes that produce berries or fruit. These nasty guys can totally defoliate a bush in a couple of days. You can obliterate them by removing the nest and immersing it in soapy water (dish soap will do the trick) or by blasting them with a good, hard spray of the hose until they've all washed away. Or you can use the simple, old-fashioned method favoured by my father: roll a newspaper, light the end, and burn the nest off. Just be careful not to ignite the rest of the bush or the surrounding area!

Gypsy moths hitched a ride to North America on plants imported from Europe and Asia in the 1860s. The caterpillars of these moths feast on deciduous trees, weakening and even killing them. The trees most likely to be affected are oak, cherry, white birch, maple, alder, willow, and elm. Many municipalities have launched spray campaigns to control gypsy moths.

Here's how to recognize the gypsy moth in its various stages. The eggs can be found in late fall or early spring on trees or nearby buildings. They're found in a hairy, whitish mass that can contain more than 300 eggs. The caterpillar is dark and about 4 to 7 cm (1 1/2 to 3 inches)

Tent caterpillars can pick trees clean in a few days. If you spot them on your property, blast them with a hose or burn them off—very carefully!

long, with a series of spots down its back: blue spots near the head and red near the tail. They become pupae in late June or early July and emerge as moths a week or two later. The adult gypsy moth is dark brown with black bands across its wings.

The following are some steps you can take to prevent gypsy moths from infesting your property:

* Keep trees as healthy as possible by making sure they are well watered. Protect the base of the plant with mulch to conserve moisture and keep lawn mowers and weed-control tools away from the tree: any damage to the base can stress the tree, making it an easier victim for gypsy moths.

* If you notice egg masses on your tree, remove them immediately. You can scrape the eggs off with a trowel or dull knife or you can vacuum them off quite easily. I recommend using a Shop-Vac—just empty it into the garbage when you're done. (Your neighbours may think you've taken cleanliness to a new level if they see you vacuuming your trees, but it works!) If you remove the eggs by hand, squish them by stomping on them or immerse them in a bucket of soapy water (again, dish soap is perfect) to be sure they are dead.

* Wrap a 15 cm (6 inch) band of duct tape around the tree, about about 1 to 1.5 metres (4 to 5 feet) above ground level. Slather the tape with Tanglefoot, a sticky material available at your garden centre. This will stop the caterpillars from travelling up the tree.

* You can also stop the caterpillars by wrapping your tree with burlap. Tie some twine around the middle of the burlap and fold the top half over the bottom half. As the caterpillars crawl up the trunk at night, they will become trapped. In the morning, you can remove them and kill them by stomping on them or by immersing them in soapy water.

If your trees have been affected severely by gypsy moth caterpillars for at least one year, consider using Btk. This is a biological insecticide: it's a bacterium that attacks butterflies and moths in the larval (caterpillar) stage. Btk is not harmful to humans, birds, or other animals because it targets only the gut of these larvae. The leaves must be covered well by the spray, as it is effective only as the young caterpillar feeds. You can apply Btk yourself or hire a professional. Btk can also control tent caterpillars, but several applications are required. Keep in mind, though, that Btk will eliminate most caterpillars in the area you're treating—even desirable ones, like those that go on to become monarch butterflies. For that reason, use products like Btk as a solution of last resort.

You may notice tiny green, red, or black insects crawling on the new, tender growth on your plants: these are probably aphids. For now, I suggest just washing these guys off with a blast of the hose. If they keep coming back, however, you may need to take more drastic action. See the Summer chapter (page 173) for complete details on how to deal with aphids.

Wrapping the trunks of trees with burlap can prevent gypsy moth caterpillars from climbing them.

**Spring** Flower Garden

# VEGETABLE GARDEN

## Your spring vegetable garden checklist:

✔ When danger of frost has passed, plant bean, corn, and squash seeds.
✔ Choose your favourite varieties of tomatoes and peppers.
✔ Protect your strawberry plants and get set to pick the first crop.
✔ Take steps to keep your vegetable garden clean and healthy to deter diseases and pests.
✔ Buy or build a composter.

In early spring, you prepared a garden plot in a location receiving full sun and with easy access to water. You amended the soil with rich organic matter. You made a list of the vegetables your family likes to eat and considered the amount of space you have available. If you planted radishes, lettuce, or other cool-season crops in early spring, you may already be enjoying your first salads! Now, as the season progresses, your vegetable garden will kick into high gear.

## Planting Your Vegetables

When all danger of frost has passed and the soil has warmed up, you can start planting seeds for tender crops. That includes most beans, corn, cucumber, kohlrabi, pumpkin, squash, and zucchini.

Read the label to determine how far apart you should plant your seeds. However, when sowing smaller seeds, I like to plant them close together in continuous rows and thin them out later. For example, if the package says to space the seeds 5 cm (2 inches) apart, plant them much closer than that and then thin out the weakest sprouts, leaving at least 5 cm (2 inches) between those that remain. Larger seeds should be sown in groups of two or three, increasing the chances that at least one will be successful—and if all three germinate, just keep the strongest. I'm a huge fan of seed tape—strips of biodegradable material that contain vegetable seeds evenly spaced to make your job super-easy. You just lay the tape in the soil at the right depth, cover it with soil, and water the planting. (You'll still need to thin out the weakest sprouts.)

Plant seeds a little closer together than the packaging suggests. After they sprout, thin out the weakest ones.

Finally, in the case of some vegetables, it makes more sense to buy them as plants from your garden centre. (You could have started these from seed earlier in the spring, but I suggest you buy the plants instead of spending time and money on seeds, soil, boxes, and sun lamps.) Celery, eggplant, peppers, broccoli, Brussels sprouts, cabbage, cauliflower, and tomatoes are best grown this way.

Keep in mind the rules about height that we discussed in the Early Spring chapter—taller plants to the east or north—and leave ample space between plants. Most veggies need to be grown in rows 25 to 45 cm (10 to 18 inches) apart, but some need even more space, so plant for future growth. Broccoli, Brussels sprouts, cabbage, cauliflower, cucumber, eggplant, potatoes, squash, Swiss chard, and zucchini need at least 50 cm (20 inches) between rows, and pumpkins need at least 2 m (7 feet) to spread out!

Weeds are sure to turn up as uninvited guests. You'll also want to guard against dryness, bugs, and disease, so visit your vegetable garden regularly to do a quick inspection and pick weeds as soon as they appear. You can uproot them with a hoe, but be careful to pull the weeds by hand if they are growing close to your vegetable plants.

## Frankie's Tip

Squash and pumpkins are fun to grow, but they take up a lot of space in the garden. Before you try to plant them, make sure you have the room: one zucchini plant can easily take over an area of about a third of a square metre (4 square feet), and a pumpkin plant needs at least 1 square metre (about 10 square feet). Squash needs full, direct sun and constant monitoring for diseases like powdery mildew.

2047
9.0327-74
GROWN IN CANADA
CULTIVÉ AU CANADA

Many vegetables are easier to plant as seedlings. Just make properly spaced holes with your fingers or a small trowel, drop in the seedling, and pack firmly.

Make sure you leave lots of space between your rows of vegetable plants. If you're new to vegetable gardening, it helps to label the young plants (*left, top and bottom*). If you prefer to sow from seed, seed tape (*above*) is the easiest way to ensure you get vegetables in perfectly spaced rows.

Mulch is a sure-fire remedy for weeds, as well as a way of retaining moisture in the soil. Almost anything can be used for mulch in the vegetable garden: commercial mulch from your garden centre, leaves, grass clippings, hay, landscape fabric, or even newspaper weighed down with stones. As a bonus, adding mulch to your vegetable garden helps your tomatoes and cucumbers stay clean by keeping them away from the soil.

## Tomatoes

Nothing tastes better than a tomato from your backyard sliced up in a sandwich for lunch! I said earlier that one tomato plant can feed a family of four, but you can never really have too many tomatoes. Cherry tomatoes for the kids, beefsteaks for sandwiches and stuffing, Roma to-

Nothing beats a sliced garden-fresh tomato on a sandwich or a hamburger!

matoes for sauce, and don't forget some Early Girls so you can start eating sooner. Any uneaten ripe tomatoes can be turned into sauce or washed and thrown in the freezer for future use.

### Frankie's Favourite Tomatoes

#### Better Boy
Slabs of this tasty, mid-size tomato are great in sandwiches and on burgers. About 75 days.

#### Big Beef
Vigorous and disease resistant, these large beefsteak tomatoes won't crack. About 75 days.

#### Brandywine
This heirloom variety matures late and produces large, imperfect fruit, but the flavour will keep you coming back. My favourite tomato for Caprese salad. About 90 days.

#### Caspian Pink
This large Russian heirloom tomato is a beefsteak type, packed with flavour and great sliced or in salads. About 80 days.

#### Early Girl
A medium-sized and tasty tomato that I like because it's the first one you get to harvest! It begins to produce fruit in as few as 52 days after planting.

#### Roma
An Italian favourite that's great for sauce. It's also my choice tomato for summer salads. About 70 days.

## San Marzano

The supreme plum tomato, San Marzano has fleshy fruit that's perfect for pasta sauces. It performs best when staked. About 80 days.

## Sugary

These super-sweet grape tomatoes, each with a distinctive pointed tip, grow in clusters. Kids love them! About 60 days.

Plant your tomatoes on an overcast day—or in late afternoon if the day has been hot. Otherwise, your plants will wither and take longer to establish themselves. As you dig the holes, allow for a space of 45–90 cm (18–36 inches) around each plant. Toss a handful of well-rotted manure into each hole, add water, and let it soak in before planting. I also recommend adding some crushed eggshells to the soil for the calcium they provide.

Then fill the space around the plant with soil and press down firmly. (Don't worry about planting too deeply, as new roots are produced along any portion of buried stem, making the plant stronger.) After planting, remove the bottom pair of leaves and give each plant a stake for support, being sure to tie it very loosely. I prefer to put a tomato cage in place at this stage instead of a stake: that way it is already in place when each branch becomes heavy with tomatoes.

Water well with lukewarm water and keep the soil moist. Each tomato plant requires 3 to 4 litres (about 1 gallon) of water twice a week, so if it hasn't rained at least 2.5 to 7 cm (1 to 3 inches), drag out the hose. If an unexpected frost is called for, cover your plants with newspaper, a light sheet, or plastic overnight. (Make sure the plastic doesn't touch the leaves.) To protect a small plant you can just place an overturned bucket on top of it. Mulch at the base of each plant to conserve moisture and protect from weeds. To keep whitefly and other insects out of your tomatoes, you can plant a row of marigolds—a natural and pretty way to keep the bugs away. Fertilize if your soil is lacking nutrients: look for a plant food specially made for vegetables.

Get into the habit of monitoring your tomato plants. Good soil, full sun, lots of water, and a little maintenance will help them flourish:

* As the stem thickens and more leaves appear, "suckers," or side shoots, will show up in the crotch between the stem and the branches. Pinch these off. Otherwise, the suckers will become new branches and the plant will put energy into producing more foliage instead of the beautiful tomatoes you want.

* Give freshly formed flowers a good shake to spread the pollen, which will increase fruit production.

* As the season progresses, guide the plant through the wire cage to support the ever-heavier branches.

* Remove any brown or withered leaves or any leaves showing blackspot, a fungal disease caused by damp, humid conditions. You can control blackspot by removing the affected leaves or by spraying with an organic fungicide.

Plant your tomatoes a little deeper than soil level, covering the bottom of the stem (*above left*).

To encourage a tomato plant to devote its energy to bearing fruit, pinch off the suckers that grow in the crotch between the stem and the branches (*above right*).

Build a tomato support system! A wire cage (*left*) will support your growing plant when it starts producing, and a row of marigolds can help deter some insects.

*Get Growing*

# Peppers

In much of Canada, peppers are not a great choice for the vegetable garden. They take a long time to mature and they need a lot of heat: the fewer growing days and the lower temperatures at northern latitudes mean that the chances of having a great crop of peppers is small. If you really want to grow them, look for varieties like 'Northstar', a bell pepper that's ready in 66 days.

Peppers need to be planted when the soil is warm. Remember, soil temperature is much slower to change than air temperature, so one or two sunny days isn't enough. Gardeners of yesteryear used the "bare bum test": they dropped their pants and sat down on the soil, and if it was warm, then it was time to plant. I suggest using this method only if you have a fenced-in yard!

When planting your peppers, dig a hole 10 cm (4 inches) deep, throw in a handful of well-rotted manure, and mix with a teaspoon of Epsom salts to provide magnesium, a nutrient essential to pepper plants. Add water to the hole, and when it has soaked in, plant the pepper and fill the hole, pressing the soil firmly around the stem. Pepper plants should be spaced 30 cm (12 inches) apart.

To encourage your pepper plant to branch out and grow bushy, pinch off the top pair of leaves when two or more pairs have grown.

Fertilize with compost or organic fertilizer when your pepper plant first flowers and then again about three weeks later. As with tomatoes, plant marigolds nearby to keep the aphids away.

Pick your peppers as they are ready: the more you pick, the more the plant will produce.

Peppers are delicious and easy to grow, but they need to be planted late in the season when soil temperatures are warm. Be warned that they can take a long time to mature.

*Spring* Vegetable Garden

# My Favourite Vegetables to Grow in Containers

No space for a vegetable garden? No experience growing your own food? No problem. One of the best ways to get your feet wet is by growing vegetables in containers. That way you can see if you really enjoy it before you spend all that time and money building a vegetable bed. When you plant vegetables in containers, use potting soil, which is light and retains moisture. Since potting soil is lacking in nutrients, however, you'll need to fertilize your plants once every week or two: use a general-purpose plant food or one designed for vegetables

• tomatoes (cherry tomatoes are great for kids!)
• peppers
• leaf lettuce
  (grow these in a long, narrow window box)
• radishes (these can grow in a box too)
• eggplants
• cucumbers (look for varieties designed for
  containers, or use vine-type varieties and
  stake them)
• pole beans
• green onions
• most herbs, but especially basil and parsley

Radishes (*top right*) and romaine (*bottom right*) are among the earliest crops in the spring vegetable garden and can be easily grown in containers.

# Strawberries

There's nothing sweeter than strawberries grown in your own backyard! If you already have strawberry plants in your garden, you should get your first crop of berries sometime in late spring.

As flowers begin to appear on your strawberry plants, keep only those produced on nice, thick stems. Pinch off any that appear on weaker stems so the plant's energy can go toward producing fat fruit on the thicker ones.

Continue to mulch your plants with fresh straw. This will retain moisture by keeping the sun's rays off the soil, and it will discourage weeds from growing. As the plant begins to produce fruit, the straw will also keep the berries off the ground so they stay clean and dry, reducing the chances of rotting.

Your strawberries will need protection from rabbits, squirrels, and birds—everything loves strawberries! Netting will work if your pesky intruders are not too aggressive. Blood meal sprinkled around that section of the garden should also scare them off.

If you notice your flower buds dropping off, you may have an infestation of strawberry weevil. A couple of good sprays with an organic insecticide is the only way to combat them. If you notice your fruit being nibbled by bugs, you probably have sap beetles. They're attracted to the ripe fruit, so pick the berries as soon as

Pick fruit only when it's at the peak of ripeness. This strawberry isn't quite ready yet.

they are ready. You can trap the beetles in a larger yogourt container by covering the bottom with mashed ripe fruit, then planting the container in the garden with the rim at soil level. Discard any trapped beetles by dumping them into a bucket of soapy water.

## Protecting against Diseases and Pests— Naturally

Every gardener has to contend with plant diseases and pests at some point. A little preventive medicine can go a long way toward keeping your garden healthy so you won't have to use chemicals.

* Keep the soil nutrient rich and well drained for maximum plant health. Adding compost or well-rotted manure to your existing garden soil will help roots grow vigorously, producing a strong plant that can resist disease and the ravages of insects.

* Take care when selecting plants for your garden. Don't buy plants that appear to be damaged by insects or disease. Instead, choose varieties that are resistant to these things. Native plants are a good choice: they thrive under local conditions and have acquired resistance to local pests and disease.

* Maintain your garden with the correct amount of water. Water deeply in the morning so moisture does not stay on the foliage (since it will evaporate with the heat of the sun).

* Prune large, overhanging branches from mature trees to admit sunlight and improve air circulation.

* Keep the garden area clean and as weed-free as possible. Remove dead or decaying plants: they attract disease and provide shelter for insects.

* Cover the soil with mulch. Be sure to use clean, weed-free mulch to discourage weeds and help retain moisture.

* Practise crop rotation where possible, to combat insects and disease that can remain in the soil.

* Monitor your garden regularly for early signs of trouble. Check the foliage closely, examining both sides of the leaves of plants that are not thriving. On the top side, look for obvious damage, which can range from spots to chew marks. On the bottom side, look for bumps, which could be insect larvae. Remove leaves that show any of these signs.

* Protect and attract beneficial animals such as ladybugs, bats, and toads, all of which feast on harmful insects. You can buy ladybug lures, bat houses, and even "toad abodes" to encourage these friendly creatures to come to your garden.

* Investigate methods of companion planting to prevent insects from attacking your plants. For example, plant nasturtiums near cucumber plants, since the cucumber beetle will eat the nasturtiums before going after your vegetables. Leafy plants such as lettuce are protected by planting radishes nearby: bugs will eat the radishes first. Marigolds planted at the base of tomatoes help to repel a bunch of insects.

A row of marigolds along a raised bed can help keep bugs and animals away—besides, it looks great!

 **Spring** Vegetable Garden

The best composters in your garden are worms! Earthworms consume decaying plant matter and return it back to the soil. Gardens populated with worms will be rich in organic matter and nutrients, and they'll be well aerated and have good drainage—all of which adds up to great plants. You can put worms in your composter to speed up the process—you can even buy them online and have them shipped to you!

No matter how hard you try, insects are bound to appear eventually. But before heading out to your garden centre for remedies, simply remove the bugs by hand and squash them, or remove the affected portion of the plant. You can also simply wash the varmints off with a good stream of water from your hose. You'll have to do it a few times, but this method usually works quite well. If these steps fail, you may need to take more drastic action. Identify the offending insect or disease and look for products designed for that specific problem. Choose one labelled as safe for children and pets.

## Composting

As well as producing lots of good things to eat, your vegetable garden will also create a lot of organic garbage. If you have room in your yard, consider starting a compost pile. Not only will you have a place to discard your garden waste, but you'll be creating a natural, nutrient-rich soil amendment. The process takes about six months to a full year before the compost is ready to be spread in the garden.

Composters need heat, oxygen, and water to produce certain bacteria and fungi that will break down organic waste. You can buy a composter from your garden centre or home improvement store, and some municipalities make them available free of charge or at low cost. Although they tend to be small, they are tidy and do the job well. Another option is to make your own. You can enclose your compost pile in wood or wire or you can just heap it on the ground and cover the pile with a dark plastic tarp.

Keep in mind these composting tips:

* Most composters you get from municipalities are on the small side—they still work, but if you can, try to make your compost pile at least 1 square metre (9 square feet) in area.

* Put your composter in a location that will receive full sun, if possible, as heat from the sun will speed up the decomposition process. A dark plastic cover on a homemade compost heap will also retain heat.

* Along with waste from your garden, you can include kitchen scraps, teabags, coffee grounds, eggshells, and dryer lint. This is your "green" material, which is rich in nitrogen.

* Cover this green material with a layer of "brown," carbon-rich material. This includes dried leaves and grass clippings, ashes, hay, and small twigs. Finally, add a layer of soil. The soil contains the bacteria that help the organic matter decompose.

* To accelerate the natural breakdown, chop or shred any material you add to your composter.

* Do not compost meat, dairy products, animal waste, bones, or shells from seafood. These items may attract animals and other pests, not to mention the terrible odour they create.

* Don't put weeds or diseased plant material in the composter.

* Every few days, or after each new addition, mix the pile with a shovel. This adds air to the compost and helps eliminate odours.

* Keep the compost moist but not wet. Ventilation and mixing will help dry out a soggy pile—as will the addition of more brown material.

* You know your compost is ready to spread if it clumps slightly when you squeeze it.

 **Spring** Vegetable Garden

Composting is natural, but you can improve your results by helping the process along. Chop up large pieces of plant and vegetable material and give the pile an occasional turn with a garden fork (*above left*). Layer the pile with nitrogen-rich greens (*above right*) and carbon-rich browns. Add a few handfuls of soil (*left*) to supply the microorganisms that kick-start the process. If the pile dries out, add water to get things moving again (*facing page*).

*Get Growing*

# LAWN

## Your spring lawn checklist:

✔ Mow your lawn at least once a week, keeping the grass between 6 and 8 cm (2 1/2 and 3 inches) high.
✔ Water and fertilize only if necessary.
✔ Attack dandelions by pulling them out at the root before they have a chance to go to seed.
✔ Rake and remove moss from problem areas and take steps to make sure it doesn't return.

If you fertilized your lawn in early spring, you'll probably question whether that was such a good idea. The cool temperatures and frequent spring rains certainly make that grass grow fast—and the dandelions too. Get set for a season of mowing and weeding!

## Mowing

Cutting your lawn is a weekend ritual in spring—in fact, you may need to cut it more than once a week.

Mowing the lawn may seem simple, but there is actually a right and a wrong way to do it. Grass should be kept to a height of 6 to 8 cm (2 1/2 to 3 inches). Leave the cuttings on the lawn, where they will break down and provide nutrients—a natural, chemical-free way to add nitrogen. Not to mention that you're saving yourself a lot of work by not having to rake it.

Don't be tempted to lower the blades, even though keeping the blades higher will likely mean you'll be cutting the grass more often. Cutting the grass too short reduces its ability to maintain root health. Strong, healthy roots spread deeper, giving your lawn drought tolerance, vigorous growth, and great colour. You might want to relieve the boredom of the lawn-mowing job by cutting in a different direction each time: this also offers the benefit of spreading the clippings over the lawn more evenly. To avoid clumping—and to reduce wear and tear on your mower—mow only when the grass is dry.

## Watering and Fertilizing

It's not usually necessary to water your lawn in spring. But in the event of very dry weather, give the grass a good, deep watering: 2.5 cm (1 inch) per week. Morning watering on a windless day makes for the most efficient use of our precious water resources.

A healthy lawn usually needs fertilizer only in early spring and again in the fall. However, if you're repairing a damaged lawn or if you just want to create a beautiful, green spread, you may want to add another application at this time. If you want to do this, look to organic, slow-release fertilizer that will provide the nutrients your lawn needs without adding more chemicals.

## Dandelions

I know the feeling: the grass is looking great until that warm day in May when your lawn suddenly becomes a golden sea of dandelions. The best way to keep dandelions under control is to take action before they colonize your property.

First, fertilization and proper cutting will keep your grass growing vigorously and will crowd out many weeds.

Although it sounds tedious, removing dandelions by hand can be very effective. Try to get on this task early, as it is far easier to pull out a few small plants now than to let them grow, germinate, and spiral out of control. You have to get the entire root. If you don't, a new plant can come up from the old root. To make this easier, attack after a rain, when the ground is softer. You may also find it's well worth investing in one of the many gizmos that help you pull dandelions without having to bend over each time.

If removing dandelions seems impossible, at the very least, pick off the flowers so they don't produce seeds. Cutting the lawn in spring before the dandelions have a chance to flower and produce seeds is an easy way to do this.

As a last resort, where legal, herbicides are available to rid your lawn of weeds. In areas with pesticide bans, new products appear every year. Chelated iron is one that works well: it weakens and eventually kills broadleaf weeds but doesn't harm grass. The best way to find out what works in your area is to talk to your neighbours who don't have dandelions—just make sure whatever they're using isn't banned!

Finally, learn to accept that life is not perfect and neither is your lawn. Just do the best you can.

My favourite dandelion puller is a weed's nightmare: just stick it into the soil around the root (*top left*), squeeze the prongs together, and pull the whole thing out (*top right*)! You can also attack dandelions with a handheld trowel or weeding tool (*bottom left*). Just make sure you remove the whole root (*bottom right*) so the weed doesn't return stronger than ever.

*Get Growing*

Other common lawn weeds: black medic (*top left*), broadleaf plantain (*top right*), creeping charlie (*left*).

Moss tends to grow in areas that receive little light and where the soil is acidic and/or compacted.

*Get Growing*

# Moss

You may find moss growing on your property under trees or in areas with compacted soil, poor drainage, very little light, and/or poor air circulation. It may bug you, but I have come to like it. It covers the soil in areas where it's difficult to fit a lawn mower.

If you do want to get rid of moss, ammonium sulphate will eradicate it: look for a 21-0-0 product with a coverage of about 4.5 kg (10 lb.) for every 90 square metres (1,000 square feet). Commercial moss killer is also available: it contains ferrous sulphate and ammonium sulphate. After about two weeks, rake the dead moss and remove it.

However, moss will grow back if the same conditions continue to exist. Aerating soil and providing more light and air by pruning surrounding trees can prevent it from appearing again. Reseed the area with a grass seed that's suited specifically for shade. If moss is occurring near evergreens, acidic soil may be part of the problem, which you can correct by applying lime.

### Frankie's Tip

You may not want moss on the lawn, but on rocks and on rustic-looking clay pots, it's a beautiful thing! Try this trick: put a handful of moss and 500 mL (about 2 cups) of plain yogourt into a blender. Then paint the mixture onto your rocks or pots. Keep them in the shade and use a spray bottle to keep them moist. Within a week, the spores from the moss will begin to grow on the bacteria from the yogourt!

When you've finished all your spring tasks, take some time to step back and enjoy your plants. Late spring is one of the best times in the garden: ample rain and cool days help everything thrive. Now your job is to keep things looking this good as the weather gets hotter and drier—and buckle up because here comes summer.

# Playing Defence

**Y**ou'll know your garden is in its summer phase when the days are getting longer and the lilacs have faded, replaced by the blooms of coneflowers, phlox, butterfly bush, and hydrangea. And those impatiens and petunias you planted in spring have finally filled in the bare spots in the garden beds. In the vegetable garden, lettuce and radishes will be ready to harvest. You'll also notice some less-welcome signs of summer: insects and disease have moved in.

If spring was about preparation and planting, summer in the garden is really a time of survival. Most people think that winter is the season that kills plants, but summer is much more deadly. Weeds attempt to suffocate your prized perennials; aphids attack your roses; and hot, dry weather can severely weaken your plants. When I worked in the garden centre, sales in our "plant pharmacy" went way up in summer because it is the season of blackspot, bugs, and slugs.

My goal in this chapter is to guide you through the challenges of summer. So slap on the sunscreen, pick up those pruners, roll out that hose, and let's get started!

# FLOWER GARDEN

**Your summer flower garden checklist:**

✔ Prolong blooming with regular deadheading.

✔ Prune spring-flowering shrubs such as lilacs.

✔ Keep the garden as weed-free as you can, taking special care to remove weeds before they produce seeds.

✔ Fertilize perennials about once every four weeks but only until midsummer.

✔ Support plants with stakes or trellises as necessary.

✔ Water and fertilize containers and arrange to have them looked after if you go on vacation.

✔ Use responsible watering practices to avoid waste and to make your plants more drought-tolerant.

✔ Do some troubleshooting to figure out why certain plants are struggling.

✔ Look for ways to keep your yard cool, such as planting a shade tree or adding a water feature.

✔ Cut flowers and bring them indoors to enjoy.

✔ Watch for signs of insects and take steps to control them.

✔ Examine your plants for diseases and treat or discard the plants or parts of them as necessary.

*Get Growing*

# Deadheading

I know it sounds vicious, but it's really not. Deadheading is the removal of spent flowers on annuals and perennials. Plants naturally focus most of their attention on their fruits, flowers, and seeds, so removing flowers that are past their glory allows the plant to refocus its energy on producing additional buds, more blooms, and longer periods of colour.

So how do you deadhead? All you need to do is remove the spent flower and its stem by pinching them off with your fingernails (if the stem is thin) or cutting them off with scissors or pruners. The task can be tedious, but it's worth it: the more you deadhead, the more blooms you'll get.

Delphinium, coreopsis, and most varieties of spirea (including 'Goldflame', 'Goldmound', 'Anthony Waterer', and 'Little Princess') require more than deadheading: they need aggressive pruning. After delphinium and coreopsis have finished blooming, cut them back to about 10 cm (4 inches) from the ground. Cut spirea back by about a third, and within a few weeks, presto, you'll get another series of blooms. If you're nervous about cutting back that much, stick to my rule of thumb: you can't go wrong if you prune by one-third.

### Frankie's Tip

*A word to the wise— don't teach your toddler how to deadhead. I thought it would be a fun way to get my son Matheson involved in the garden, but now he just pulls out plants all over the place!*

When deadheading small, tender plants, you don't need pruners. You can simply use your fingernails or a pair of scissors.

If you're lucky enough to have rhododen-drons or azaleas in your landscape, deadheading is essential because it helps with the production of the next year's blooms. If you don't remove the spent flowers, you'll run the risk of minimal bud production, meaning fewer flowers for next year.

Stop deadheading, pruning, and fertilizing your roses in midsummer. This limits the amount of tender, new growth that won't be hardy enough to survive the winter.

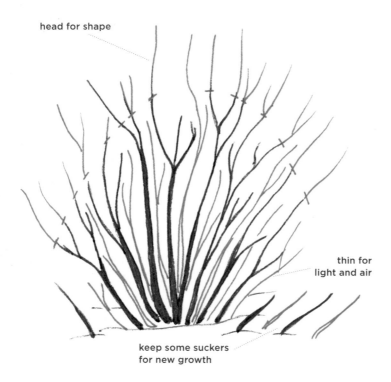

head for shape

thin for light and air

keep some suckers for new growth

Lilacs and most other shrubs can be pruned back (or "headed back") by one third after they have bloomed. Selectively thinning branches to admit more air and light can prevent powdery mildew and disease. Remove suckers at the base of the lilac only if you don't want the plant to spread.

# Pruning Spring-Flowering Shrubs

**B**y now you'll likely remember my rule: "Prune after bloom." And, true to this guideline, early summer is an ideal time to give spring-flowering shrubs a little horticultural hairdressing. Actually, it's the only time to prune lilacs, since they take an entire season to develop their flower buds: if you prune a lilac too late, you will remove next year's flowers.

If you have mature lilacs on your property, I recommend attacking them in stages as shown in the following list. These steps can be applied to any deciduous or flowering shrub:

* Prune out any dead or diseased wood, cutting stems back to the live wood or right back to the ground.
* Prune back the oldest woody stems. These are usually thick, dark, and woody in appearance. Cut them so that you shorten the overall height of the shrub by no more than a third at any one time.
* Remove any inward-growing branches.
* Pinch off any remaining spent flowers.
* Clear the area under the plant of any fallen stems, branches, and leaves and water deeply.

You may be wondering, "Can I limit the size of a plant by constantly pruning?" You *can* control some plants with frequent pruning, but the chances of your taking a 'Skyrocket' juniper and controlling its height to a couple of metres are slim: you'll most likely kill it before you control it. Forcing a plant to fit is like trying to make a young child sit still.

*Get Growing*

# 7 Reasons Why That Plant Isn't Blooming

### Not enough sun

Sure, your mock orange used to bloom with glory, but that was before that maple to the west of it was shading your area. Over time, certain locations may become more shaded due to trees maturing or new structures being built (such as a neighbour's shed).

### Improper pruning

Lilacs and rhododendrons are just two examples of shrubs that take an entire growing season to develop new buds. If you prune them too late in the season, you'll remove next season's flowers.

### Too much nitrogen

If your plants are nice and green but aren't blooming, there may be an overabundance of nitrogen in the soil due to improper fertilization. Broadcasting lawn fertilizer in the garden can create all green, no bloom.

### A late cold snap

Early warm-ups followed by late visits from Jack Frost back in the spring may have frozen flower buds.

### Planting too deep

When the eyes of a peony are planted too deep, you will not get flowers. If your peonies fail to bloom but everything above seems to be doing well, grab your spade or fork and lift the peony tubers so the eyes are about 3 cm (1 inch) above soil level.

### Transplant stress

When you move or transplant a flowering plant or shrub, you'll give it a little shock. Sometimes the plant will cope by focusing energy on its root system, and it may not flower during the first year as it gets re-established.

### It's just a late bloomer

Wisteria, trumpet vine, and a few other flowering vines can take a few years before they establish themselves and start blooming. Be patient—these plants are worth the wait!

## Frankie's Tip

Okay, I'm in weather-guy mode now. When gardening in the summer, it's important to protect yourself. Gardening is good exercise: one hour burns an estimated 272 calories (based on a 68 kg [150 lb.] person), or the equivalent of a grande caramel macchiato from Starbucks! But to avoid injury, do some stretching before and after your work. Keep yourself hydrated by drinking lots of $H_2O$, and slather on the sunscreen. Sunstroke and heatstroke are common in gardeners who are careless during the summer months.

2047
9.0327-74
GROWN IN CANADA
CULTIVÉ AU CANADA

## Weeding

If you thought you had your fill of weeding during the spring, I've got bad news: the fun continues all summer too. In early summer, plants haven't really filled out yet, so there's still a lot of exposed soil in the garden, with just the right amount of light to germinate weed seeds. Weeds amaze me—they seem to thrive in places where you can't get anything else to grow!

Here are some tips for controlling summer weeds:

* The best time to weed a garden is when it's damp—either after a rain or following a morning watering. When the ground is moist, it's much easier to remove the roots.
* Don't just pinch off the top. The more of the weed you can remove, the smaller the chance it will come back.
* A thick layer of weed-free mulch (it doesn't matter what type) can reduce weeding by up to 90 per cent. Laying down mulch is also an excellent way to retain soil moisture during the hottest months.
* Remove weeds before they flower and set seed.
* When removing weeds that have gone to seed, be careful not to broadcast the seeds. Immediately place them into a closed container or yard disposal bag.
* Avoid placing weeds in your composter. If you put the weeds in, you'll end up putting the seeds back in your garden later.
* Use a spade to maintain a good edge around garden beds or use some type of edging to keep lawn weeds from creeping into the garden.
* If a sunny area of the garden is overrun by weeds, suffocate them by placing a black tarp or plastic sheet over the soil. The tarp will restrict light, moisture, and oxygen and cook the weeds in the summer sun.

Weeds will not go away on their own, so set aside some time in your summer schedule for this task. You can reduce the workload by staying on top of the problem in early summer!

## Staking

Plants are like people: the older they get, the more support they need. As the growth in your garden takes off in the warmth of summer, some of your plants may need to be staked.

Staking helps plants stay upright making them look tidier and helping support fruit or flower heads that are just too big to hold up. It also maintains health by keeping foliage off the ground and allowing good air circulation. Peonies, hollyhocks, dahlias, zinnias, tomatoes, pole beans, and peppers may all require staking.

**Frankie's Tip**

Continue to give your perennials, trees, and shrubs a general-purpose plant food once a month or so until midsummer. But stop fertilizing after that: by late summer you want their top growth to slow down as the plants prepare for the upcoming fall and winter. A late flush of growth stimulated by fertilizer could be harmed by an early hard frost.

*Get Growing*

Your battle against weeds continues all summer. Stay on top of the job so weeds don't take over.

**Summer** Flower Garden

Nylon stockings are ideal for securing plants to stakes—they're sturdy but flexible, so they allow your plants to thrive.

You can use store-bought plant supports like peony rings, obelisks, and tomato cages or you can just make your own from old hockey sticks, bamboo poles, and string. When tying a plant to a stake, be careful never to use anything that will cut into the stems—no coat hangers or twist ties. String or twine will do the trick. Plant-staking clips and tape are available at garden centres, but I've found that nothing beats strips of old nylon stockings—especially if you can find green ones!

If you bought vine-type plants such as clematis, climbing hydrangeas, honeysuckle, silver lace vine, and trumpet vine, you may be looking at them now and thinking, "The tag said it was a vine, but it looks more like ground cover!" That's because most vines don't have tendrils—which give some plants the Spiderman-like ability to cling to walls or fences—so they require support and training. (Boston ivy is a Spiderman plant that doesn't require support, but be careful: it's a fast grower and may damage bricks and eaves if you let it climb up the walls of your home.) To support a vine-type plant, use a trellis, netting, or a section of chain-link fence. All

*Get Growing*

you need is something for the vine to grow through as it works its way upward—of course, the support also needs to be secure enough that the plant will not rip the entire support system off the wall.

Most vines need to be tied to the trellis with something gentle enough not to harm the stems. Over time the vine will get the idea, and then all you'll need is regular maintenance pruning to keep it growing in the direction you want it to go. You may also need to take the occasional straggler and weave it through the trellis to keep things neat.

## Keeping Containers Looking Great

At some point during the summer, you may be tempted to shout: "How come my pots don't look as good as they did at the garden centre?!" When it comes to containers, it's survival of the fittest: if your container started with eight plants, there may be only three survivors by now. That's okay—just remove the struggling ones and let the strong ones take over.

Containers, hanging baskets, and window boxes are planted in a "soilless" potting mixture that has little or no nutrient value. So if you want your plants to remain vibrant all summer, you need to apply fertilizer. I fertilize most of my containers every two weeks with a half-strength, water-soluble fertilizer such as 15-30-15. The ideal time to fertilize is immediately after a rain or right after watering: this opens up the soil and the roots so they soak up more of the much-needed plant food.

To keep a climbing vine well supported, thread the new growth through a trellis.

It's not unusual for containers to need water every day, but if you find yourself watering twice a day, your containers are too small. Larger containers take longer to dry out, so make a note to use bigger ones next year.

You will no doubt be taking a week or two of vacation in the summer, and the last thing you want to do is worry about your containers while you're gone. So what do you do? You can buy a drip irrigation system or a product like the Aqua Globe. These automatically deliver water slowly and evenly to your

To keep containers looking great all summer, water them regularly and fertilize them every two weeks. I prefer to use water-soluble fertilizers.

Going away for a few days in summer? You can make your own container waterer by punching small holes in a plastic bottle and burying it halfway in the soil. Before you go, fill the bottle with water.

containers. But here's my simpler suggestion: take a plastic bottle, drill randomly spaced holes in it, and then bury the upright bottle in the soil of your containers with only the top protruding. Fill up the bottle on the day of your departure. It may also help to group your containers together. This creates more humidity around the pots, and they may therefore dry out more slowly.

While these tips will help, there's no substitute for the human touch. If you can, ask a friend to take care of your containers when you're away—just let them know that if it rains, they don't have to come over to water.

On your return, you may well find that some containers have perished while others will need a good deadheading. You won't have time to mourn, though, because you'll be in the garden pulling out a week's worth of weeds!

## Being Water Wise

**W**atering your garden regularly will keep it looking great, but gardeners can't afford to be careless with this precious resource. Here's how you can give your garden the moisture it needs without wasting water:

### Spread on the mulch

Leaf mulch, shredded newspapers, cedar chips, river stone, or even shredded tires (treated to eliminate toxins and purchased at a garden centre)—a thick layer of 5 to 8 cm (2 to 3 inches) of mulch will conserve moisture and cool soil temperature, helping plants through hot, dry weather, not to mention reducing weeding.

### Choose drought-tolerant plants

Did you know that plants with grey or silver foliage (such as dusty miller) reflect light and typically have a greater drought tolerance than others? Plants with small, thin leaves have less surface area from which to lose moisture, and this also helps them survive in dry locations. Ask your local garden centre which plants are drought-tolerant—these usually include natives, succulents, and alpine plants.

### Roll out the barrel

Collecting rain in a barrel and using it to quench your garden's thirst during periods of dry weather is an efficient use of water. What's more, studies have shown that rain water is better for your plants than tap water. Many local municipalities offer low-cost rain barrels to encourage water-wise gardening.

### Use smart watering practices

Soak your plants, don't sprinkle! Watering plants thoroughly and infrequently will force their roots deep below the surface, and this helps protect them during hot, dry weather. Shallow watering will force roots to the surface in search of water, and this will result in a plant under stress.

A few handfuls of mulch (*top left*) can prevent plants from drying out too quickly in summer.

Drought-resistant dusty miller (*top right*)

Using a soaker hose (*above*) is an effective way to water plants slowly and deeply, which promotes healthy roots.

When you use a sprinkler in the summer (*left*), do so on a calm, windless day, and water deeply so the moisture gets right down to the roots.

Rain barrels can collect an amazing amount of water during a summer shower.

*Get Growing*

# Navigating a No-Grow Zone

In early summer, you may find that those prized perennials you planted in spring are struggling, a lilac planted two years ago hasn't bloomed, or your rose bushes are leafless. Time for some garden troubleshooting.

Before you take action, however, make sure your expectations are reasonable. You usually don't see great performance in a perennial during its first season, since the plant is just getting established. It's focusing on the roots and building a good foundation. You will usually see blooms in the second season, but often a perennial won't take off until the third year. With some plants, such as wisteria, it can take even longer to see the payoff.

If you are concerned that a perennial needs some help, ask yourself these questions:

## Is it receiving enough light?

Pay attention to plant labels, which tell you whether a plant needs full sun, partial sun, or shade. Those requiring full sun won't die in the shade, but they may not bloom. Shade-loving plants will often wither in too much sunlight.

## Is the soil too acidic or too alkaline?

Many plants don't like acidic soil. One clue to look for is evergreen needles in your garden beds: these lower the soil pH (that is, they make it more acidic) and may cause some plants to struggle. (Moss is another indication that the soil may be acidic.) On the other hand, rhododendrons bloom best when the soil is acidic—

and you can mulch them with pine needles or buy a product to help lower the pH.

## Is it planted in the right soil?

If the soil appears hard and compacted, it may contain too much clay. That may be preventing moisture and fertilizer from getting to the roots. If the soil doesn't seem to retain moisture, it may be too sandy. You can improve both problems by adding peat moss, but it's usually better to select plants that thrive in your existing soil conditions. It's easier to change the plants than change the soil!

Sometimes, even when you do everything right, plants still struggle. Often the only solution is to try something else in that location.

### Did you prune at the right time of year?

Spring-flowering shrubs bloom on last year's growth, so if you prune a lilac in the fall, you'll prevent it from blooming the following spring. Summer-flowering plants bloom on new growth, so it's okay to prune these in early spring. But don't prune them in late spring because that's when they'll be producing buds for their summer flowers. When in doubt, always remember my "prune after bloom" rule: cut your shrubs back when the spent flowers are still on the plant.

### What type of fertilizer are you using?

If you use a fertilizer with high nitrogen, you may get deep, green plants with fewer flowers. (This can happen if your broadcast spreader tossed a lot of lawn fertilizer into the garden.) To promote blooms, use a fertilizer with a high middle number (phosphorous).

### Is the plant too dry or too wet?

Some plants need moist soil and will struggle if they don't get regular waterings. At the other end of the spectrum, if you have low-lying areas in your garden, water may collect there after a rainfall, and this can cause root rot.

### Could the plant have been damaged by chemicals?

If a plant has leaves that have wilted and turned brown, a neighbourhood dog may be using it as a urinal. Or it may have been sprayed with an herbicide (that's why you should never use herbicides on windy days!) or burned by too much fertilizer.

### Have the roots been damaged?

If the gas or phone company has been digging on your property, they may have damaged the roots of a nearby tree.

Clay soil can get heavily compacted, preventing water and oxygen from penetrating it. If you can't improve it (peat moss can often help), look for plants that thrive in poor, acidic soil.

*Get Growing*

If a plant isn't thriving, try moving it to a new location and making a better selection for the original spot. I'm constantly moving plants around to find that perfect home for them. Ideally, you shouldn't do this in summer, but if you have to, choose a cool, overcast day for transplanting, to minimize the stress on the plants.

I will often move a struggling plant even if its original location is *supposed* to be suitable in theory. I've learned to accept that some plants just will not grow in certain locations even if you have the right amount of sun, you've improved the soil, and you've taken the time to prune and fertilize. Sometimes this is because of things we can't see—like wind patterns or what is happening below the ground.

Here's another common problem: many homes have a roof that extends past the walls of the building and overhangs the garden. Plants under this overhang may not get watered in a rain shower, and they may get very little light.

Finally, when I have a spot where nothing will grow, I'll often resort to putting some decorative mulch there and adding a nice container of potted annuals for colour.

## Keeping Cool

When temperatures are on the rise and humidity is building, you'll be looking to your yard as a place to relax and cool off. You don't need to spend big bucks on a swimming pool to make your yard an oasis. You can create a cool garden space by doing the things I've described below.

### Plant deciduous trees for shade

Proper placement of shade trees not only cools your yard, but can also reduce your air conditioning costs by shading south- and west-facing windows. The benefit of deciduous trees is that they lose their leaves in autumn, allowing the sun to warm the house through the same windows during the winter.

### Add a water feature

Install a table-top water garden, a statue and fountain, or an elaborate waterfall. The sight and sound of flowing water creates an enjoyable, cooling effect—though it may have you going to the bathroom a little more often!

### Pay attention to colour

Choosing flowering plants with cool, soft colours makes for relaxing spaces. Hot colours such as red, orange, and hot pink make great poolside attractions.

### Improve air circulation

Sometimes you need to kick a few plants aside to cool off your yard. Overgrown garden spaces—especially those surrounding the property—prevent the flow of cool crosswinds. This isn't usually a problem in suburban areas, but I see it all the time in the city, where small yards are surrounded by mature trees and shrubs. If your plants are continually diseased, prune or remove some of them to create additional airflow and circulation.

A pond can have a calming, cooling effect in a garden in summer.

*Get Growing*

This space has a lot of beautiful plants, but it's too crowded (*top*) and needs a little "garden editing." I've removed many of the plants (*bottom*) so that the remaining ones will thrive.

 **Summer** Flower Garden

# Attracting Hummingbirds to Your Garden

Hummingbirds are a symbol of summer gardening and undoubtedly the coolest creature on the planet! They are the only birds that can fly forwards, backwards, up, down, and sideways and hover in midair. They have the largest brains of all birds (as a percentage of body size) and their little hearts beat over 1,200 times per minute!

You can attract hummingbirds to your garden by keeping it chemical-free and paying attention to their favourite things:

**Favourite type of flower:** Those with tubular shapes, such as petunia, fuchsia, foxglove, bleeding heart (*below*), and nicotiana

**Favourite food:** Nectar and small insects

**Favourite colour:** Red (a great red-flowering shrub is 'Bristol Ruby' weigela)

**Favourite place to feed:** Close to a tree, since hummingbirds are shy and need a place to hide

**Favourite place to cool down:** Moving water such as a fountain or sprinkler

# Bringing the Garden Indoors

**O**ne of the best ways to savour your garden is to bring it indoors. Cut flowers are a great way to celebrate summer with an explosion of colour. But not all of your garden blooms make good cut flowers: you'll want to select varieties that will last a long time in a vase. See the next two pages for some of my favourites.

Cut flowers during the coolest part of the day or on overcast days. I like morning best. Use a sharp pair of scissors or shears to make a clean cut. Immediately place the cut flower into a bucket filled with room-temperature water. When cutting the flowers in the garden, be selective so the plant still has good garden appeal.

Once indoors, cut off the bottoms of the stems and remove any foliage from their bases to make sure no leaves touch the water in your vase. For flowers that have large hollow stems, place a cotton ball into the stem. This may help retain moisture.

To make your cut flowers last as long as possible, place them in a room with indirect light, away from vents. Use a clean vase, change the water frequently, and remove any spent or rotten blooms and stems to make the bouquet last as long as possible. I also recommend buying small packets of floral preservative at the garden centre or florist and adding it to the water. You can also add half a teaspoon of bleach per litre (per quart) of water to help kill bacteria. (You'll often hear that adding sugar to the water will help cut flowers, but it won't. Save it for your coffee!)

I like to cut flowers in the morning, while it's still cool. Place them in a bucket of water immediately and don't let them dry out. Once inside, arrange them in a clean vase, then step back and admire them!

**Summer** Flower Garden

# Frankie's Top 5 Annuals for Cutting

clockwise fom top left

**Zinnia**
**Cosmo**
**Marigold**
**Nicotiana**
**Snapdragon**

# Frankie's Top 5 Perennials for Cutting

clockwise fom top left

**Shasta daisy**

**'Pacific Blue' delphinium**

**Black-eyed Susan**

**Phlox**

**Coneflower**

# An Ounce of Prevention

Before we look at all the different insects and diseases that can attack your garden in summer, let's consider a few ways of heading off these problems before they start:

**Use your hose as a weapon.** You're walking through your garden and you notice that one of your favourite perennials is being attacked by insects. What do you do? How about grabbing the hose? One of the fastest ways to rid your plants of insects is simply to blast them with a high-pressure spray (*below*). This won't eliminate them, but it will give you time to find a solution before they counterattack. Before you turn the hose on them, however, grab a few of the insects and the leaves they're attached to and place them in a sealed container. Then take them to the garden centre or your friendly neighbourhood horticulturalist for identification.

**Take time to smell the roses**—and inspect your plants at the same time (*above*). Check the leaves (including the undersides), stems, buds, and blooms for markers indicating pest problems such as holes, chew marks, blistering, or struggling foliage. Look for disease markers such as black spots, white film, or fungus.

**Water properly.** One of the best ways to minimize the risk of disease and insect problems is to water in the morning and thus prevent water from pooling on leaves. Morning watering allows for the most efficient use of water—plants have time for absorption but then the afternoon sun gets rid of any excess moisture that could cause disease. If you water in the evening, the garden stays wet for too long, since the sun cannot evaporate water overnight.

# Bugs and How to Control Them

You may think that no one is as fond of your garden as you are, but unfortunately that's not true. Insects and other creepy crawlies love your plants even more—and they outnumber you! To protect your plants from bugs, inspect the plants regularly and try to figure out what type of insect is to blame for any damage. Then you can target that species with a technique or a product that's safe and effective. (To learn more about the insect-control products mentioned here, see "The Plant Pharmacy" on pages 187–88.)

## Ants

**Signs:** Small sand mounds in the garden, between patio stones, or at the edge of the driveway.

**Identification:** You know what ants look like. However, the ant you usually don't see is the queen, who lays eggs during the warm summer months to keep the colony going. Ants eat everything from leaves and food scraps to decaying wood, but their favourite food is nectar and aphid honeydew.

**Control:** Typical garden ants don't kill plants. (Don't worry if you see them on your peonies: ants love the nectar on peony buds, and they do no harm to the plant or flower.) However, ants can build mounds in your garden that can weaken and even kill nearby plants. If an ant mound is not too close to a plant, try slowly pouring boiling water onto it. You may need to do this more than once for complete success, but it does work. You can also create your own bait stations with a 50–50 mixture of Borax and sugar. Keep these small: use the lid of a small jar or something similar. The sugar is the attractant, and the Borax is the secret weapon: worker ants will take the mixture back to the colony, eventually feeding the queen and ultimately destroying the colony. Plants that repel ants include catnip, peppermint, sage, and spearmint. (Note: Carpenter ants, which typically nest in decaying wood, rather than gardens, can cause severe damage and should be treated by a professional pest control company.)

## Aphids

**Signs:** New growth appears stunted or struggling; curled leaves; lack of blooms; overall appearance of plant is tired.

**Identification:** Aphids have tiny, soft, pear-shaped bodies and may be white, green, black, or red. If you have ants on your plants, you may have aphids too. That's because aphids leave behind a secretion called "honeydew," which ants like to feed on. Look for aphids on the undersides of leaves and on flower buds and new growth.

**Control:** If you spot aphids, immediately wash them off with a high-pressure spray from the hose. Insecticidal soap and neem oil will also control them. Plants that repel aphids include chives, garlic, fennel, dill, catnip, and marigolds. Ladybugs love to eat aphids, so you should welcome them in the garden.

Leaf miners (*above*) bore tunnels between the layers of leaves. If you can't get rid of this pest, it will eventually kill your tree. Ants do not typically harm garden plants directly, but their large mounds (*left*) can easily choke off the roots. You can often get rid of anthills using boiling water or a mixture of sugar and Borax.

*Get Growing*

## Beetles

**Signs:** Defoliation of trees, shrubs, perennials, annuals, and vegetable plants.

**Identification:** There are countless species of beetles, but only a few are particularly harmful in the garden, including the potato beetle, Japanese beetle, June beetle, viburnum leaf beetle, and cucumber beetle. All are aggressive eaters, feeding both at night and during the day.

**Control:** Controlling beetles is difficult, as their hard-shelled bodies work to protect them. Hand picking them is your first line of defence, but use gloves: Japanese beetles can get you with their pincers. Homemade insecticidal soaps (see "The Plant Pharmacy" on pages 187–88 for my recipe) work well as a preventive measure, but once you have an infestation, you'll need to find a stronger, store-bought insecticide. Plantings of garlic, larkspur, tansy, and geraniums may repel beetles.

## Cutworms

**Signs:** Soft-stemmed plants (annuals, perennials, or vegetables) are cut off at the base at or just below ground level.

**Identification:** Cutworms are the caterpillar stage of a type of moth. They feed at night and may be hard to see, though sometimes they climb the plant and feed on the leaves. Their brown to greyish bodies are soft, plump, and hairless, with a white stripe down each side. One of the easiest ways to identify a cutworm is by the way they curl up when disturbed.

**Control:** Get a good old flashlight and a bucket of soapy water and make a nighttime visit to the garden to enjoy a session of cutworm hunting: look for them near the base of your plants and just pick them off and plop them in the bucket. To prevent their attacks, you can place protective collars around the bases of plants (I use old coffee cans with both ends taken out). You can also place crushed eggshells—or the crushed shells from the mussels you ate last night—at the base of the plant to create barriers for any crawling insect. Nematodes, which can be purchased at garden centres and are used for killing grubs, will also attack cutworms.

## Leaf Miners

**Signs:** The blistering of leaves, especially on birch trees; leaves that are papery, translucent, and so thin that their layers can be peeled apart.

**Identification:** Leaf miner is the larva of various insects that live and feed inside the leaf of a plant. If you examine the leaves closely, you'll notice the black pellets these larvae leave behind as they tunnel through the leaves.

**Control:** Because the leaf miner creates a home inside the leaf, spraying insecticide is useless. The only effective remedies are "systemic insecticides," which are absorbed though the bark and roots. Unfortunately, these are not readily available if you live in an area with a pesticide ban. You may have no choice but to remove the infected branches and discard them. If you have three seasons of severe leaf miner infestation, you'll probably have to remove the tree.

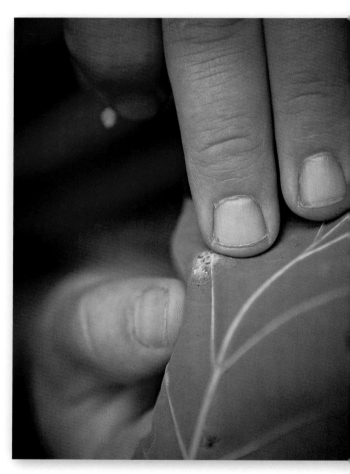

Beetles are voracious, and once they've infested your plants they're difficult to get rid of.

Mealybugs leave a white, cotton-like substance on leaves. These scaly little insects can suck the life right out of your garden plants.

*Get Growing*

## Mealybugs

**Signs:** A white, cotton-like substance on leaves; yellowing leaves; leaf drop.

**Identification:** Mealybugs are small, light-coloured, scaly insects with sucking mouth parts. They are often covered with a white, waxy coating. Like aphids, they secrete honeydew, which can lead to mould growth. Not only do mealybugs suck the life out of your plants, but they also harbour disease. Their favourite plants include chrysanthemums, geraniums, begonias, primula, gladiolus, Boston ivy, Virginia creeper, coleus, and yew.

**Control:** Mealybugs are not easily controlled. Predator insects are the best way to keep their numbers in check, including ladybugs and green lacewing. (You can actually buy these insects online and have them shipped to you.) You can try insecticidal soap or use a cotton swab to rub the bugs with alcohol. But if a plant is severely infested with mealybugs, I recommend removing and discarding it!

## Red Lily Beetles

**Signs:** Remarkably fast defoliation of Asiatic lilies.

**Identification:** The red lily beetle is easy to spot: it's about 8 mm (3/8 inch) long, with a bright red body and a black head and legs. The larvae have dirty-orange-red bodies with black heads: they usually cover themselves with their own slimy black excreta and could be mistaken for bird droppings. If you turn over the leaves of the plant, you'll often see their dark-coloured eggs in a straight line. They attack only Asiatic lilies, not day lilies or other types of lilies.

**Control:** As soon as you see a red lily beetle, "pick and squish" as fast as you can, as these little critters can be aggressive eaters. If you see the eggs under the leaves, just squish them with your fingers. Neem oil may also be effective in preventing them and killing them if they've already arrived. Unfortunately, these beetles are very difficult to control, and many gardeners in affected areas have just stopped growing Asiatic lilies.

## Scale Insects

**Signs:** An overall weakening of trees or shrubs; discoloration of foliage; a sticky substance on leaves, making them appear glossy.

**Identification:** Scale insects are often immobile, so they can be difficult to spot. They're usually found on stems and appear to be hard bumps or tiny, disk-like shells. Underneath this shell is a sucking insect that feeds on the juices of the plant. Trees and shrubs affected by scales include cedar, azalea, birch, box elder, euonymus, honey locust, juniper, magnolia, oak, pine, and yew.

**Control:** You can remove scales simply by flicking them with your nail, using rubbing alcohol on a cotton swab, or even using an old toothbrush. Pruning out the infected areas may also work. Predator insects include ladybugs and parasitic wasps. Insecticidal soap can also reduce scale populations.

Scale insects (*above*) can be difficult to see, as they don't move around much. Look for their disk-like shells on the stems of plants. The red lily beetle (*left*) can destroy Asiatic lilies with amazing speed. It's beautiful but voracious!

*Get Growing*

## Slugs

**Signs:** Holes in leaves and slime trails. If you have holes in your hostas, you have slugs!

**Identification:** Slugs are not insects: they're molluscs, and they're related to clams and oysters. Garden slugs are wormlike, fleshy creatures that range in size from a few millimetres to several centimetres (about 1/4 inch to 2 inches). They can lay over 500 eggs in a season, creating a whole lot of damage. The best time to spot slugs is at night or just after a light rain.

**Control:** Start by watering your garden only in the morning, so plants stay dry at night. A mulch of crushed eggshells, mussel shells, clam shells, and even wood ash placed around affected plants helps keep slugs away. But if you can't banish them, you'll have to kill them—and you may as well let them die happy! Take a shallow container (I use margarine containers) and bury it so the rim is at ground level. Now fill the container with beer. Beer attracts slugs, and they'll eventually fall into your pool of brew, get drunk, and die. The fresher the beer, the better it works—seriously! Sprinkling salt on a slug will also cause it to shrivel up and become bird food. Store-bought slug baits are available, but make sure they're safe for both children and pets before using them.

## Spider Mites

**Signs:** Small brown or yellow dots or discoloration of foliage; lack of vitality; leaf drop.

**Identification:** Spider mites are tiny, eight-legged critters, less than a millimetre (1/16 inch) long, with colours ranging from red to green to yellow. Tapping an infected leaf over a piece of white paper will help you see these little pests. You'll need a magnifying glass to see their distinctive calling card: the very faint webbing they leave on the underside of leaves and stems. Spider mites love dry heat, so they are less common during periods of high humidity and frequent rain.

**Control:** Apply a store-bought miticide (mite killer) or insecticide or homemade insecticidal soap. Reapply on infested plants at least three times, two or three days apart, to break their life cycle. If your plants are grossly infested, I suggest simply removing them to minimize the risk to surrounding plants. Onions, garlic, and chives help repel spider mites—and so will your breath after you eat these vegetables!

## Thrips

**Signs:** Discoloration of flower blooms; stunting and abnormal growth.

**Identification:** Thrips are tiny, cigar-shaped insects measuring only about a millimetre in length (less than 1/16 inch). Here's the best way to determine whether you have thrips: remove a flower or bud from the affected plant and hold it over a piece of white paper. Start removing the petals and dismantling the flower or bud. If you see a small sliver of a creature run across the paper, you've got thrips. Plants commonly infected by thrips include impatiens, petunias, zinnias, gerbera daisy, tomatoes, and peppers.

**Control:** Thrips are almost impossible to control with insecticidal soap or neem oil. All you

Holes in the leaves of your plants are a sure sign of slimy slugs. Hostas are a particular favourite of these destructive little creatures.

To make a slug trap, bury a container up to the rim and pour in some fresh beer. Slugs will be attracted to the brew and will drink themselves to death!

The easiest way to see if a plant has thrips is to pull a flower apart over a white sheet of paper. If you see tiny black insects running around, you've got thrips.

can do is try to prevent them from arriving in the first place with good garden hygiene and by keeping your space weed-free. If your plants become infested, just rip them out and replace them. The good news is that if you remove all the affected plants, the thrips won't necessarily return.

### Whiteflies

**Signs:** Clouds of tiny white bugs appear when you shake a plant!

**Identification:** Whiteflies look like tiny moths and are usually found in large numbers. They like to hide on the undersides of leaves, where they suck the juices from your plants. They can attack a wide range of targets, but they're particularly fond of tomatoes, peppers, and tropical hibiscus. Whiteflies also secrete a honeydew-like substance that can lead to mould growth on the plant.

**Control:** Whiteflies often originate in the greenhouses where your plants were grown, so inspect plants carefully when you buy them at your garden centre. If you've brought home a plant that's infested, just throw it out, rather than risk infecting anything else. Yellow sticky-tape traps can be effective in controlling whiteflies because these pests are attracted to yellow. Insecticidal soap and neem oil may also help, but you will need to apply it several times.

## The Good Guys

Not all the bugs in your garden are harmful. In fact, some are essential to the health of your plants: bees are necessary for pollination, and dragonflies, ladybugs (or lady beetles), green lacewings, fireflies, and praying mantises all eat harmful insects. Most people don't like wasps, but some species eat a lot of other insects. If you're entertaining on the deck and you want to keep wasps away, place a cup or two of orange pop in the garden. The wasps will have a feast and leave you and your guests alone!

Not all insects are garden pests. Ladybugs can keep your plants healthy by feasting on aphids.

Moisture and high humidity can lead to blight, especially on tomatoes and potatoes.

Blackspot is a fungal disease that is especially harmful to roses.

*Fusarium* (wilt) is a deadly disease that can't be treated. The best way to avoid it is to purchase plant varieties that have a resistance to it.

*Get Growing*

# Diseases and How to Control Them

As if bugs aren't enough to contend with during the summer, your garden will also have to take a stand against plant diseases. Prevention is your best weapon in the battle against fungal diseases: proper watering techniques and good air circulation will go a long way toward keeping your plants disease-free.

## Blackspot

**Signs:** Exactly what you'd expect from the name: round black spots on leaves, eventually causing yellowing and leaf drop.

**Identification:** Blackspot is a fungus, and if you look closely, you'll notice the tiny spores: these can overwinter on both stems and fallen foliage, so the blackspot returns the next season. This disease can weaken shrubs to the point where they lose all their foliage and eventually die. Several plants can be infected with blackspot, but roses are the most common victim.

**Control:** Blackspot loves moisture, so keep your garden dry by watering only in the morning and pruning to ensure good airflow. Immediately remove any infected leaves, whether they're on the soil or still on the shrub. Remove the bottom leaves of rose bushes so they don't pick up fungus from the ground. You can purchase fungicides that are effective, but they may need to be applied several times during the growing season. If you're planning a new rose garden, consider varieties that are resistant to blackspot, such as the Canadian Explor-er series, 'Knock Out', Flower Carpet roses, or some of the David Austen varieties.

## Blight

**Signs:** Fuzzy, patchy growth; wilted leaves; brown or discoloured foliage; rot.

**Identification:** Blight is a disease caused by mould. It commonly occurs on flowers and vegetable plants—especially potatoes and to-matoes—after periods of moisture and high humidity.

**Control:** Blight is easily spread and can be fatal to plants, so controlling it is very important. It's best just to remove any diseased plant. That may seem drastic, but you're sacrificing one for the benefit of others, which is better than losing your entire crop. Don't water in the evening, and keep water off the foliage by staking or using tomato cages and mulching with clean straw. As a last resort, apply a fungicide.

## Fusarium (Wilt)

**Signs:** Yellowing or blackening of leaves, followed by leaf drop and a rapid weakening of the plant.

**Identification:** *Fusarium oxysporum* is yet another type of fungus that won't rest until it destroys your tomato crop. Sometimes called "wilt," it causes the leaves on your tomatoes to turn yellow or brown and droop.

**Control:** Wilt is a terminal disease, and fungicides are not effective on it, so good gardening habits are your best defence. Keep areas

free of debris and decaying plant material, use mulch around tomato plants, and keep water off foliage. Remove any diseased plants immediately. Check the tags when you buy your tomato plants and look for varieties labelled VFN, VFNA, or VFNT. The "F" in this abbreviation indicates that the plants are resistant to *Fusarium*.

## Powdery Mildew

**Signs:** Foliage coated with a greyish-white powdery substance; overall weakness of the plant.

**Identification:** Powdery mildew is most likely to occur during periods of damp followed by high humidity. It reproduces through spores that can overwinter on affected plants. Powdery mildew can occur in almost any plant, but some are more susceptible, including lilacs, phlox, bee balm, crabapple, squash, and cucumber.

**Control:** Poor airflow, overcrowding, and improper watering can all lead to a bad case of powdery mildew. To minimize the problem, plant your garden leaving enough space for adequate airflow, prune regularly, and water only in the morning (keeping water off foliage). Remove diseased sections and be sure to sterilize your shears with bleach after pruning. Don't fertilize until you have mildew under control, since the fungus is attracted to new shoots. As a last resort, use a fungicide, which may need to be reapplied if the fungus persists.

## Rust

**Signs:** Orange or reddish-brown spots or lesions; stunting and disfigurement; leaf drop; overall weakness of plants. One variety (cedar-apple rust) produces large, spiny growths called "galls."

**Identification:** Rust is another type of fungus, and the orange-red colour of the spots it leaves is the best way to identify it. Hollyhocks, hawthorns, roses, asters, snapdragons, and crabapples often get rust. The cedar-apple variety often attacks junipers.

**Control:** Avoid watering foliage, leave ample space between plants to ensure good airflow, and keep gardens as clean and weed-free as possible. Mallow (a type of weed) is particularly vulnerable to rust, which can then spread to other plants. Remove infected foliage and discard it to prevent the rust from overwintering and reappearing. In areas where rust has appeared in the past, applications, twice a month, of a fungicide during the growing season may help prevent it.

Powdery mildew can spread quickly on lilac, phlox, bee balm, and other plants.

The best defence against rust and other fungal diseases is to keep water off the leaves and avoid watering plants at night.

# The Plant Pharmacy

Good garden hygiene—removing weeds, cleaning up debris, paying attention to airflow, selecting resistant plant varieties, and proper watering—is the best way to steer clear of harmful insects and fungi. But when preventive measures fail, sometimes you need to get out the big guns. Garden centres carry a range of products that will help you control bugs and diseases, and many of these are chemical-free.

**Baking soda** is an effective homemade fungicide. Just combine 5 mL (1 teaspoon) of baking soda with 1 litre (4 cups) of water and a few drops of liquid dish soap and spray plants liberally.

**Btk (*Bacillus thuringiensis*)** is a bacterium that is toxic to the larvae of some leaf-eating insects (such as cutworms) but harmless to humans, birds, and other animals. It's available in powder or liquid form and must be applied when the insects are feeding. It needs to be reapplied at one- to two-week intervals and after rain.

**Diatomaceous earth (DE)** is a naturally occurring powder that includes the fossilized remains of tiny aquatic creatures called "diatoms." Applying DE is an old method of controlling bugs in crops, and it's not harmful to humans. It's effective against beetles, ants, aphids, and whiteflies: insects that come into contact with it become dehydrated and die. It can also deter slugs. Sprinkle it on plants in the morning, when they're wet with dew, so the dust will stick to the leaves.

**Insecticidal soap** coats the shells of bugs, making it impossible for them to breathe. But it must be sprayed directly on the insect to be effective. It is completely harmless to humans and pets. Always use it during the cooler part of the day or on an overcast day, as it can burn leaves if applied in the hot sun. It is effective against aphids, spider mites, Japanese beetles, mealybugs, caterpillars, and whiteflies. You can make a homemade version of insecticidal soap by dissolving 5 mL (1 teaspoon) of liquid dish soap in 1 litre (4 cups) of water.

**Neem oil** is a botanical pesticide that comes from the neem tree (*Azadirachta indica*) of South Asia. Neem oil stops young insects from maturing and it also makes plants taste bitter, which makes even the young bugs stop eating them. Any mature insects that arrive on the plant from elsewhere are also repelled by the bitter taste. Neem oil needs to be sprayed weekly—and after every rain—as long as evidence of infestation exists. (Warming the neem oil slightly helps it mix with water for spraying.) Neem oil is effective against aphids and whiteflies. It is also an effective miticide (mite killer) and can even control fungal diseases. It is harmless to humans and animals and to beneficial bugs such as butterflies and bees.

**Pyrethrin** is an organic insecticide extracted from the chrysanthemum plant. It is non-toxic to humans and pets, yet it kills a wide spectrum of insects. It leaves no residue, and it breaks down after one day. However, it may be harmful to birds and beneficial insects, so it should be used only when no other remedy is effective. (It's best to use it in the evening when bees are less active.)

**Rotenone** is another botanical insecticide, which is extracted from the roots, seeds, and leaves of certain legumes. It is widely effective against caterpillars, whiteflies, aphids, beetles, and flies. Rotenone should be used with caution, however. Never use it near fish ponds, as it is toxic to fish. It's also toxic to beneficial bugs and can affect humans. Rotenone breaks down in sunlight, so apply it in the evening when the air is still and bees are inactive.

**Sulphur** is deadly to many fungi—including blackspot, powdery mildew, and rust—as well as mites. Many solutions containing sulphur are available: spray them on foliage at the first sign of disease. The treatment may have to be reapplied if the disease persists or reappears later in the season.

Insecticidal soap (*top*) works by suffocating, so it needs to be applied directly on the insects to be effective. Do your best to cover both the top and bottom of the leaves (*bottom*).

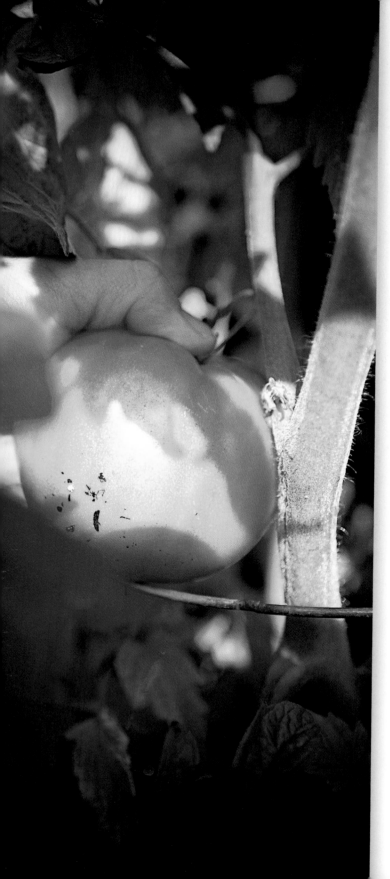

# VEGETABLE GARDEN

**Your summer vegetable garden checklist:**

✔ Harvest early crops such as radishes and lettuce and keep harvesting to encourage production.

✔ Use techniques such as succession planting and intercropping to make the most of your garden space.

✔ Maintain your vegetable garden by thinning seedlings, weeding, watering, and fertilizing.

✔ Protect your crops from damage by making the garden unattractive to animals.

Now that it's summer, you can finally enjoy some of the fruits (and vegetables) of your labour! This is when you can harvest some of your cool-season crops and plant new crops to replace them. It's also time to protect your plants from the elements so you can continue to enjoy fresh garden vegetables all summer long.

## Enjoying an Early Harvest

If you planted some early-maturing vegetables in the spring, you'll be ready to start harvesting during the first weeks of summer.

Root vegetables can be picked early in the summer and eaten when they're still small and tender. Baby, or bunch, carrots, as well as early

Onions are ready to harvest when their tops turn yellow and fall over.

beets, are all good in salads at this time of year. You can also cut the foliage from your beet plants and enjoy them as "beet tops." Carrots and beets will continue to grow larger all season, so you can harvest them throughout the summer and into the fall.

If you're planning to grill your zucchini, pick them when they're only about 15 cm (6 inches) long or so. If you let them grow very large, they'll get tough, and then they'll only be good for zucchini loaf.

Harvesting Swiss chard is like giving the plant a haircut: it keeps growing back. In fact, the best way to make sure you have a healthy, happy, and long-lived crop is to encourage growth by continual harvesting. Allowing any vegetable crop to ripen too long will weaken the plants and ultimately lead to some rotting, which creates conditions for disease. This is especially important with most herbs and those crops that continue to produce all season—like Swiss chard and most tomatoes.

Always wash and inspect your harvest before eating it. You never know when a bug or slug might be hiding in the leaves or whether it's been pretested or contaminated by a neighbourhood pet or, in the countryside, a night-prowling animal. If you've sprayed your vegetables, wait at least a week before harvesting them. Some chemicals—and even some organics—may leave a residue on the food that could be harmful.

Salad days! All your hard work in the garden is rewarded at harvest time.

*Get Growing*

Mint (*top left*) is an easy-to-grow perennial herb that thrives in poor soil. Warning: mint is so easy that it may take over your garden! Rosemary (*top right*) and parsley (*above*) are favourite herbs that grow well in containers.

**Summer** Vegetable Garden

No space for a vegetable garden? These eggplants (*top left*) were grown in recycling boxes.

Keep harvesting Swiss chard (*top right*) all season long. The more you cut it, the faster it grows back.

Beans (*left*) are among the first vegetables in the ground in early spring, and one of the earliest crops to harvest.

# Your Garden Game Plan

If you really want to get serious about having a continual harvest, consider these two techniques.

The first is succession planting, or replacing harvested crops with new ones. This is one of the best ways to maximize the output of a small space. One example is planting radishes in early spring, followed by a planting of squash in early summer, and then another crop of radishes or spinach in late summer or early fall. (Both the early spring and fall crops must be frost-tolerant.)

Here are some crops you can use when succession planting:

| Early Spring | Early Summer | Late Summer/ Fall |
|---|---|---|
| Radish Kohlrabi Turnip greens Eggplant | Squash Tomato Pepper | Beet Spinach Swiss chard |

Intercropping is another way to maximize your space in the vegetable garden. Intercropping is a method of planting faster-growing vegetables between those with longer maturity dates. For example, radishes planted between rows of cabbage: the radishes are harvested well before the cabbages get big and need that space. Broccoli and Brussels sprouts also take longer to mature, so you can grow a quick crop like radishes or bok choy between them. Or try fast-growing lettuce as an intercrop around tomatoes and summer squash.

Finally, always remember the importance of crop rotation. Even if you're doing intercropping or succession planting, make sure you plant root crops, squash, and leafy vegetables in locations that are different from the locations used for the previous planting—as much as you can. (That is, plant squash where root crops were last planted, put leafy vegetables in the former squash patch, and plant root crops where the leafy vegetables were last time around.) This will not only replace nutrients in the soil (because the new planting will not necessarily use the same nutrients that the previous one used). It will also reduce the likelihood of spreading disease, since, for example, pests that go after root crops might not go after squash.

## Maintaining Your Vegetable Garden

Harvesting is the fun part of summer vegetable gardening. Enjoy it while you can because pretty soon it'll be back to work!

If you sowed vegetables by seed, you'll improve your results by removing the weakest seedlings. This eliminates overcrowding and ensures that the stronger plants survive to produce a healthy harvest. Some new gardeners have trouble with the idea of pulling out plants, but trust me, you're sacrificing a few for the greater good!

Before your vegetable plants really take off in summer, there is a period where a lot of soil is exposed, which is ideal for the germination of weed seeds. Mulching with clean straw—or using the handy newspaper trick described earlier, on pages 61–62—will help, but the best thing

To ensure a healthy crop, thin out weak and straggly seedlings, leaving behind only the strongest.

 **Summer** Vegetable Garden

is to set aside some time for weeding. A weed-infested vegetable garden will produce a disappointing harvest because of the competition for resources and lack of airflow. Regular weeding also reduces insect problems and diseases.

Watering is critical during the hot summer months. There are three key ideas to remember: water in the morning; water deeply and infrequently; and keep water on the roots and off the foliage. Irregular watering results in diseases like blossom-end rot, which causes dark, hardened patches to appear on the bottom of your tomatoes. (To control it, just remove and discard any affected tomatoes.) It can also cause vegetables to split and often makes them taste bitter. Allowing plants to dry out will stress them, causing them to drop their blossoms and stop producing more.

If you've invested in good soil before planting in spring, your garden will need little to no fertilization. But for poor soils or if you're trying to grow vegetables in containers, fertilizer will help with the harvest. Vegetables typically enjoy a fertilizer with a ratio of 1:2:1—for example, 15-30-15 or 5-10-5.

Regular weeding in the vegetable garden means your plants won't have to fight for resources.

*Get Growing*

If you want to feed your plants without chemical fertilizers, try these homemade recipes:

### Coffee grounds
Used grounds provide an excellent source of nitrogen when used as a soil amendment.

### Compost tea
Take a scoop of compost, place it in cheese-cloth, and allow the "teabag" to steep in water for 24 hours.

### Fish water
Cleaning the fish bowl or tank? Dilute the dirty fish water at a ratio of one part fish water to two parts clean water and use it as a fertilizer.

### Milk
Have a few drops of milk left at the bottom of the bag? Fill the bag with water and apply this mixture to your tomatoes. The calcium will promote growth and prevent blossom-end rot.

### Potato water
After you boil your potatoes or pasta, let the water stand and cool, then use it to water your plants. Potatoes and pasta are rich in starch, which most plants enjoy!

### Wood ash
Save the ashes from your fireplace in winter and use them as a "soil sweetener" in summer. Ash helps increase the alkalinity of the soil (that is, makes it less acidic). Using it around plants like beets, cabbage, and cauliflower will not only help improve their growth but also help keep crawling insects and slugs away.

Blossom-end rot in tomatoes (*top*) is often the result of irregular watering and a lack of calcium in the soil. When your milk bag is almost empty, fill it with water and pour the mixture on your tomato plants (*bottom*). The calcium can help prevent blossom-end rot.

Kids love to grow and eat cherry tomatoes—even big kids like me!

*Get Growing*

And here are some other quick tips that will keep your vegetable garden producing well:

* Remove suckers (side shoots) from tomatoes. (See pages 131–32 for instructions.)
* Remove seed heads from rhubarb to improve plant health.
* Remove flower heads (also known as scapes) from garlic to improve the size of the bulb. You can eat the scapes—enjoy them fried or steamed!

## Protecting Your Veggies from Animals

I'm a fan of wildlife—rabbits, deer, raccoons, squirrels, birds, and even skunks and mice. However, in the vegetable garden, wildlife can lay waste to all your hard work. How do you keep these unwanted guests out of the garden without harming them? Play with their senses! If you can make your garden look threatening, sound scary, smell like an enemy, feel unpleasant, and taste awful, I can almost guarantee the neighbourhood diners will move elsewhere. Let me give you a few examples:

### Sight

The scarecrow is an old tradition in the vegetable garden, but truthfully, they don't work that well. However, an owl statue (plastic or concrete) will scare away everything from bunnies to birds. Why? Because owls eat bunnies and birds! The key is to move the owl around on occasion—if you don't, the birds and rabbits will just think the owl is too lazy to get them.

### Sound

Deer typically feed at dusk and dawn. Placing a radio or alarm clock in the garden and programming it to turn on at these times may frighten them away. I've had better success with talk radio—music stations just get the deer bopping!

### Smell

The scent of humans and dogs will keep many critters at bay. Human hair or dog hair placed around prized plants leaves the smell of fear, scaring away rabbits and deer. (For some reason, squirrels and raccoons just don't care.) The other benefit: when the hair breaks down, it adds nitrogen to the soil.

### Touch

I don't know about you, but stepping on sharp objects usually makes me walk in the other direction. The same holds true for most animals in the garden: place the stems of prickly plants such as roses and barberry on the ground around your plants. Be careful, though—you may not want to do this if you have children or pets who wander.

### Taste

How does this sound: two rotten eggs and 5 ml (1 teaspoon) of hot sauce mixed into a litre of water? Sounds pretty awful, and it is. The U.S. Forest Service has used a similar mixture to deter deer from eating young trees. You can try mixing this up in a blender and spraying it on your plants—if you can stand the smell!

A well-placed owl statue will often scare off rabbits and birds that cause damage in the garden. Just be sure to move it around occasionally, or the animals will catch on!

*Get Growing*

# Keeping Cats Away

Cats don't exactly qualify as wildlife, but they can make a mess of your garden: cats treat exposed areas of garden as huge litter boxes. The key to making sure that felines stay away from your plants is to cover those open spaces.

**Plant up exposed areas.** Simply adding some annuals in the empty spaces can deter feline intruders.

**Cover the area with coarse mulch or stone.** The rougher, the better, as cats have sensitive paws.

**Zest them.** Cats hate the smell of citrus, so grate the rind of lemons, oranges, or grapefruits and place the zest in the garden.

**Scare them.** A few rubber or plastic snakes from the dollar store lying on the ground may make cats turn and run.

**Stink-bomb them.** Rue is a smelly plant that repels not only cats, but many other furry creatures, including rabbits.

**Soak them.** A little soaking with the hose or a water pistol will send cats scurrying away.

# LAWN

## Your summer lawn checklist:

✔ Minimize summer stress with proper mowing, little or no fertilizer, and regular watering.

✔ Look for signs of chinch bugs and grubs and treat as necessary.

✔ Stay on top of your weeding, being sure to remove weeds before they set seeds.

**B**lazing heat and stretches of rainless days are extremely tough on lawns. Kentucky bluegrass, fescues, and ryegrasses enjoy the cool weather of spring and fall, and they can really struggle in summer. As a defence mechanism, your lawn will naturally place itself in dormancy, meaning that its growth rate will slow and the colour will change to a yellowish brown. It's not the most appealing display, but it's important for you to know that when cooler, moist conditions return, your lawn will wake up and return to green. A brown lawn in summer is not necessarily a dead lawn!

## De-stressing Your Lawn

**H**ere are some tips to help you help your grass make it through the summer.

### Raise your mower blades

Mowing your lawn to a height of 9 cm (3 1/2 inches) during the summer (instead of the spring height of 6 to 8 cm [2 1/2 to 3 inches]) will leave the grass long enough to shade the roots. This will help your lawn retain moisture and will thus prevent scorching.

### Cut back on nitrogen

Fertilizers rich in nitrogen are ideal in spring, but during the summer, there is a greater likelihood that they will burn your lawn. If you do fertilize during the summer, look for a slow-release fertilizer designed for summer application.

### Water one inch per week

If Mother Nature doesn't turn on her tap, you just might have to turn on yours. Your lawn will remain healthy as long as it receives a minimum of 2.5 cm (1 inch) of water every week. As in the garden, water early in the day and refrain from using oscillating sprinklers, especially on windy days. They're a waste of water!

### Reduce stress

During periods of excessive heat, reduce foot traffic on your lawn. And while an inflatable plastic pool will cool your kids down, don't leave it set up for two weeks or it may kill your lawn!

## Tackling Turf Eaters

**A**s your lawn goes dormant in preparation for summer's struggles, two lurking threats may start coming to life under your green carpets.

Chinch bugs are among the most common lawn-damaging insects, and their handiwork is most notable during the summer. These

sap-sucking critters announce their appearance with brown circles in the driest areas of your lawn, especially on slopes and at edges. If you notice these brown areas sometime after July, you likely have chinch bugs. An easy way to confirm this is to take a white towel and lay it on the dead areas of grass: if the chinch bugs are there, within minutes, you'll see the small reddish or black things hop onto the towel.

There are several ways to control chinch bugs:

* Pray for rain! Chinch bugs can be washed away and will remain inactive during wet weather.
* Apply insecticidal soap early in the day or in the early evening. Apply weekly for a period of three weeks.
* Crazy but true: use your Shop-Vac! As soon as you spot a damaged area, rake it (to disturb the bugs) and then vacuum them up and toss them in the garbage. Water the area thoroughly afterwards to minimize stress.
* Where they're legal, chemical insecticides are available to control chinch bugs.

Grubs are the larval stage of beetles: if you see Japanese beetles or June bugs hitting your outdoor lights on summer nights, you can be certain that grubs are near. These squirming pests are white to yellowish wormlike creatures with brownish heads. They feed on grass and grass roots and have been known to chew on garden plants as well. Grub damage is easy to spot: irregular brown patches of lawn that will lift in your hands because the grubs chew right through the roots. If you're digging in the garden or if you lift up sod, you'll probably find grubs. If you find six or more in a 900 square cm (1 square foot) area, you should be concerned.

Chemical controls for grubs work well, but they are now banned for residential use in many parts of Canada. But there are several other ways you can control these pests:

* Wet weather will keep grubs at bay, and your lawn will grow at a healthy speed, so grub feeding will remain unnoticed.
* Burying a piece of potato for a few days can attract grubs. Then you can harvest the grubs and toss them—potato and all—into a bucket of soapy water.
* Nematodes (or roundworms) are a type of biological control that can be purchased from your garden supply centre. They come stored in a sponge, which you submerge in water to release them. Follow the package instructions to apply them after a rain or thorough watering. The nematodes travel through the soil and enter the bodies of the grubs, eventually killing them.
* Milky spore, applied in a way similar to the method used for nematodes, is a bacterium that is harmless to humans and pets but lethal to grubs.

If you have bare patches in your lawn because of grub damage, do your best to repair them now with pieces of sod. If you don't, weeds will quickly move in to fill up the patches for you!

*Get Growing*

One of the best clues that you've got a grub problem is turned-up patches of lawn like this one—evidence that raccoons or other animals have been digging for this tasty treat.

**Summer** Lawn

## Staying on Top of Weeds

**F**inally, while summer is a stressful time for your grass, it's the ideal season for the production of weed seeds. The flower heads of weeds mature and produce seeds, sending them off with a mission to germinate on your lawn. That's why it's vital to stay on top of weeding during the summer months: be diligent in removing weeds from both lawns and gardens before they set seed. This will dramatically reduce your weeding as the season progresses. Unfortunately, there's only so much you can do: your neighbours may not be as diligent as you are, and a strong wind will make their weed problem yours!

**By the time summer winds down, your lawn and garden—not to mention you—may be showing signs of fatigue. That's not surprising, as you've all been through some difficult months. But as the evenings get longer and cooler and the bugs finally disappear, you'll be ready to enjoy my favourite season in the garden. Bring on the fall!**

Weeds will bring you to your knees in summer! Pull them out by the roots, and stay on top of the job to prevent weeds from taking over.

# Final Fling

**F**all is my favourite time of year. It's the season when Mother Nature puts on her final fireworks display of the year—the last blast of colour before the whites and greys of winter set in. As the trees change from green to yellow, orange, and red, the garden will offer some autumn cues as well: summer-flowering plants are slowing down and fading, and asters and stonecrops are coming into bloom. The threat of overnight frost is back, and many birds have already left for warmer destinations. A sure sign of the season is that garden centres will be selling pots and pots of mums.

I like to think of fall as a reward for enduring the challenges of summer. You worked hard to keep bugs, drought, and disease from taking their toll on your plants, and now you get to reap the benefits. As temperatures cool, your plants won't be under as much stress, so you won't have to babysit them. And, of course, you'll be able to harvest that bounty of vegetables you've been waiting for!

Fall can still be busy: you'll be cleaning up after summer's celebration of blooms, planting bulbs for next spring, running to the garden centre for some great deals on perennials, and protecting your garden from the winter weather that's on its way.

# FLOWER GARDEN

## Your fall flower garden checklist:

✔ Replace tender annuals with frost-tolerant varieties such as pansies and mums.

✔ Plant bulbs such as tulips and daffodils for a brilliant spring display.

✔ Dig out and store tender bulbs (such as gladioli and tuberous begonias), so you can replant them next spring.

✔ Divide spring-flowering perennials or plant new ones.

✔ Take advantage of fall discounts to stock up on perennials and garden supplies.

✔ Plant new trees and shrubs up until a few weeks before hard frost.

✔ Winterize your roses by protecting the crowns and roots.

✔ Prune deciduous trees (except maple and birch) to control their size and shape.

✔ Consider adding plants with all-season interest.

✔ Bring tender plants indoors for the winter.

✔ Prepare your garden for winter: stop fertilizing, cut back spent perennials, and protect vulnerable plants from heavy snow, winter burn, and hungry wildlife.

✔ Turn off and drain outdoor taps and sprinkler systems and cover any garden structures that may otherwise be damaged by ice.

✔ Store fertilizers, chemicals, and garden tools.

*Get Growing*

# Frost-Tolerant Shots of Colour

As the cooler fall weather approaches, take a walk through your garden with a critical eye. Are your petunias looking leggy and tired? Are your containers droopy—maybe even a bit depressing? After a long, hot summer, your garden may need a boost to finish off the growing season. A trip to the garden centre will provide you with inspiration to transform your summer garden into a beautiful fall display.

Your urns and hanging baskets may already be pretty ragged. Remove any struggling plants and replace them with frost-tolerant annuals. These shots of orange, rust, yellow, and burgundy will take you into the cooler days of fall (see my list of favourites on page 213).

Things get even busier after the hard frost arrives. Many plants can survive if the air temperature dips below freezing, but when the soil freezes, that's called a "hard frost" (or a "killing frost"), and it spells doom for tender plants. The first annuals to go are usually impatiens and begonias. I actually like to remove impatiens before hard frost because they become slimy afterwards. Okay, I confess: I have actually left impatiens untouched all winter, and the next spring the only clean-up to do was to dig up the odd root clump. But that's not the right way to operate: leaving spent annuals to rot invites fungal disease into your garden. Besides, it looks messy.

Just dig each plant out, shake off the excess dirt, and discard. If the annuals produce seed—as snapdragons, cleome, and sweet peas do, for example—either leave the seed heads in the gar-

As soon as the first frost arrives (or even earlier), tender annuals are toast. Pull them out by the roots, shake off the excess soil, and toss them in the composter.

 **Fall** Flower Garden

Your summer containers will looked ragged by fall. Update them with mums, kale, and other autumn showpieces.

*Get Growing*

den or give the plant a good shake before discarding and you'll be rewarded with new plants in the spring. Place these spent annuals in the composter—as long as they are not diseased—and fill the empty spaces in your garden beds with frost-hardy annuals and perennials.

Here are my fall favourites. All of them work in both containers and garden beds.

### Asters

These perennials, which produce daisy-like flowers in shades of pink and purple, look great in urns all summer. When they start to look a little ratty, you can plant them in the garden in late fall. Prune them and they'll come back next spring. If your asters were already in the garden all summer, a late-summer pruning will promote fall bloom and control height.

### Fall pansies

Available in a rainbow of colours, pansies are the tried-and-true flowering annual for fall. They are biennial, and some fall varieties will bloom again next spring before dying.

### Garden chrysanthemums

A fall staple, available in hundreds of varieties, all exploding with colour. Mums are frost-hardy, but they rarely survive winter in most areas.

### Ornamental cabbages and kales

Garden centres now offer a huge number of varieties of these members of the *Brassica* family. They produce amazing foliage—often in white, pink, and purple—and the colour looks better and better as the temperature drops.

### Sedum

Available in trailing ('Blue Spruce') or upright varieties ('Brilliant' and 'Autumn Joy'), these hardy perennials may overwinter in a container.

Asters

Fall pansies

Garden chrysanthemums (*top*), ornamental cabbage (*bottom*)

*Get Growing*

Sedum (*top*), ornamental kale (*bottom*)

## Planting Spring-Flowering Bulbs

Nothing draws you into the garden in spring like a splendid display of crocus and daffodils. The range of colours, heights, and flower types is vast, the cost is affordable, and the payoff is bloomin' awesome! If you want a beautiful spring display, fall is the time to plant bulbs.

Before heading out to the garden centre, take a few moments to sketch a rough plan. Most bulbs do best planted in an area that receives morning sun because light shade in the afternoon will allow the blooms to last a little longer. As with most plants, bulbs require fertile, well-drained soil.

Here are some tips for placing them:

* For early bloomers such as crocus, scilla, and daffodil, choose areas near the entrance of your house or spots you can see from the window. A quick glance outside will remind you that spring is in the air!
* Tuck crocus near the bases of trees or near the sidewalk, so you can see them as you come and go. Plant the bulbs in the lawn, and they'll flower before the grass is green.
* You can plant daffodils in shadier spots. Remember: they'll bloom before most tree leaves have opened. In the right spot, they will happily multiply and give a better show each year.
* Hyacinths bloom a little later and fill the air with scent. Plant them near the patio or walkway, where they can be enjoyed by anyone who visits.

* Plant tulips en masse in a flower bed and then plant annuals around their spent leaves later in the spring.
* Think about allium, scilla, and fritillaria (crown imperial) to add drama to your yard. They, too, can thrive in shady spots.
* Once spring comes, you can combine your fall bulb plantings with candytuft, creeping phlox, or forget-me-nots.
* A slope, rocky spot, or woodland garden may be the ideal spot for "naturalizing." This is a method of planting bulbs where they land after tossing them, to mimic the way flowers grow in the wild. This method is used to plant crocus in lawns. Daffodils, grape hyacinths (*Muscari*), and allium also lend themselves to naturalizing.

You can achieve a formal, neat look by choosing one variety in one colour and doing a mass planting of those bulbs. Plan to buy at least two dozen bulbs of the same variety if this is the look you want. For a more casual, country-garden look, plant several varieties together. Always plant bulbs in groups of five or more of each variety and never line them up or plant them singly.

Once you're in the garden centre and picking out your bulbs, read labels and don't be afraid to ask questions. The most important rule of thumb is to choose bulbs that are large and firm with no sign of damage or mould. Remember, the larger the bulb, the larger the flower. High-quality bulbs are more expensive, but they'll be well worth the price come next spring. Take note of the height, colour, and bloom time when you make your selections. You may also want to choose scented

Planting bulbs is simple: First, break up the surface soil (*top left*). Dig a hole the required planting depth, indicated on the packaging (*top right*). Then add a layer of bone meal (*bottom left*) and place the bulb in the hole, being careful to keep it right side up! Fill in the hole (*bottom right*), pat down firmly, and water deeply.

**Fall** Flower Garden

When it comes to selecting bulbs, the rule is the bigger, the better. Look for bulbs that are firm, not mushy, and have no signs of rot.

Crocus, daffodil, and several other bulbs are well suited to "naturalizing." Scatter them randomly over a lawn, and then plant them where they land.

*Get Growing*

varieties for certain spots: blooms noted for fragrances are daffodil, narcissus, hyacinth, lily, and some tulips.

Bulbs bought too early in the fall can rot or dry up if not stored correctly. If you have bought your bulbs early (when the selection is greater), store them in a cool, dark place like your basement or fruit cellar, where they'll be dry until you're ready to plant them. Wait until your garden starts to die back and temperatures cool off before you plant your bulbs. You can put them in the ground right up to snow time.

Follow these steps for great results:

1. Prepare the area for planting by breaking up the soil to a depth of 30 cm (12 inches).

2. Dig a hole large enough to contain all the bulbs you want to plant. Be careful to make the hole the right depth, which will be noted on the package. The rule of thumb for bulbs is that planting depth should be three times the diameter of the bulb.

3. Add a layer of high-phosphorus bone meal at the bottom of the hole to encourage root growth. (Follow the directions on the box.)

4. Lay the bulbs in the hole, pointed side up and roots down. Determining the top and bottom of some bulbs can be difficult due to their shape: when in doubt, plant your bulbs on their sides and you can't go wrong! Space them according to the package directions: usually about 12 to 15 cm (5 to 6 inches) apart. Cover with soil.

5. Water the area deeply.

6. You can cover the area with leaves for mulch, but be sure to remove the mulch in early spring so you don't create a breeding ground for insects and disease.

## Storing Tender Bulbs

**C**anna lilies, calla lilies, gladiolus, dahlias, and tuberous begonias are all examples of plants grown from corms, tubers, or bulbs that cannot survive the winter. If you planted these in the spring, you can treat them as annuals and buy new ones every year or you can dig them out of your containers or garden beds, bring them indoors, and replant them next spring.

Before hard frost sets in or when the foliage dries out, carefully remove the bulbs from the ground. Brush off as much soil as possible and place them in a container labelled with the variety and colour (a shoebox is perfect—anything breathable will do). Give the bulbs an afternoon to dry, then examine and discard any that show signs of rot. Place the others in a shoebox or a paper bag filled with a dry medium, such as peat moss, perlite, vermiculite, or sand, and dust them with garden sulphur, which works as a fungicide. (Buy the fungicide at the garden centre and read the label to determine how much to use.) Store in a cool, dark place such as a basement or fruit cellar until spring. I also recommend checking these little guys during the winter and removing any rotted ones.

 **Fall** Flower Garden

You can store tender tubers and corms over the winter and replant them next spring. Dig out the tuber and cut off the remaining top growth (*left*), preferably after it has turned brown. Brush off the soil (*right*) and store the tubers in containers in a cool (but not freezing), dry, and dark place.

# Squirrel-Proofing Your Bulbs

Everyone loves fall-planted bulbs like tulips and crocuses—unfortunately, that includes squirrels, who love to dig them up and eat them. Here's how to keep these cute but destructive rodents from spoiling your spring:

- After planting, always clean up any bulb skins and other debris, as this is a marker that lets squirrels know exactly where you planted.

- Cover the soil with chicken wire: tulips will grow through it, but squirrels can't dig down past it. Unfortunately, this doesn't save your tulips in spring when they are above ground! Squirrels will sometimes eat the plants too.

- Repel squirrels by covering areas with blood meal (follow the directions on the package) or an animal repellent such as Critter Ridder. I've had success keeping squirrels away by using pelletized chicken manure. But the truth is that a hungry squirrel may just chew through the wire and kick aside the manure!

- One never-fail strategy is simply to plant bulbs that squirrels don't eat: daffodils (and other types of narcissus), allium, fritillaria, scilla, and grape hyacinth.

## Shopping for Fall Bargains

Garden centres discount everything in fall because it's far too expensive to carry nursery stock over the winter months: unsold trees and shrubs have to be moved to a sheltered area and protected from the winter elements by heavy mulching. Even then, some stock never makes it through the winter. It makes far more sense for garden centres to clear out as much as they can, so there are great bargains to be had throughout the fall season.

* Before buying discounted stock, ask whether the garden centre will guarantee them over the winter. If they will, save your receipts in case the stock doesn't survive.
* The price is right in fall, but the selection is limited. So now is the time to do a mass planting of one type of perennial.
* Friends and family may want to thin out, divide, or get rid of some perennials now. Take advantage of their offers.
* Save the seeds from annuals: sunflowers, snapdragons, cleome, sweet pea, and morning glory all have prominent seeds that are easy to collect. (Ask your neighbour for seeds from that poppy variety you love to add to your collection.) Put the flowers or seed heads into a paper bag or large envelope, give them a good shake, and then pick out the flower parts. Store the seeds in smaller envelopes in a cool, dark, and dry place.
* Shred fallen leaves with your lawn mower and leave a thin layer on the lawn as free fertilizer. Rake up the excess leaves, shred them with the lawn mower, and use them to make free compost for next spring. Collect pine needles and heap them around your rhododendrons and azaleas: the acidity will improve the performance of these plants in spring.
* Check out bookstores for discounted gardening books for yourself or to give as gifts. Library book sales and garage sales in fall are great sources for building up your garden reference library. Garage sales also offer up a supply of garden tools, accessories, and pots at rock-bottom prices.
* Home supply stores will soon be stocked with snow shovels and snow blowers that take up a lot of space: look for sales as they clear out the garden tools, hoses, and lawn mowers.

Not only is fall a time for saving money, but because of the cooler temperatures and shorter days, new plantings will need less water. Finally, all the work you do now will lead to fewer tasks during the busy spring season. That means fall is about saving money, water, and time!

## Planting and Dividing Perennials

What is the best time to plant and divide new perennials? If you answered spring, you've fallen into a common gardener's trap. The reality is that warm temperatures, greater frequency of rain, shorter days, and cooler nights make fall the perfect time to plant perennials, as well as trees and shrubs. The long, hot summer days are over and yet the soil is still warm. Those dull, dreary days of fall usually mean increased rainfall. Besides, there seems to be more time now than in spring, when we are busy planting flowers, setting up the patio, and doing a million other jobs in the garden. There's one more great reason to buy and plant perennials in the fall: they're typically discounted because garden centres want to get rid of their inventories. Jump on this opportunity!

The key is to plant early enough in the fall to allow for proper root establishment before hard frost. I strongly recommend adding transplant fertilizer or bone meal to help minimize planting stress, and always water deeply.

The horticultural rule book says that plants that bloom in the spring—such as Oriental poppies, iris, and lilies—should be divided and planted in late summer or early fall. But you can actually divide all types of perennials at this time, though it can be more difficult than in spring because of all the top growth. If you are dividing a plant that is in bloom, cut the flowers off first so the plant can focus its energy on the roots after it's been transplanted.

Follow the same instructions for dividing perennials that we discussed in the Early Spring chapter (see page 52). Remember to choose a day that is cool and overcast, preferably with rain looming. Dig around the roots and lift out the plant. Then cut the root ball in half with your spade or a knife. (If each half of the root ball is still very large, just cut them in half again with the spade.) Replant the divisions immediately—or put them in a pot to give to fellow gardeners. (Of course, plant one of the divisions back into the original location if you still want to keep your perennial there.)

Use mulch to insulate the newly divided and planted perennials. Surround the plants with a 10 cm (4 inch) layer of cedar mulch or of clean, dried leaves (you'll have plenty of this free mulch in your yard at this time of year!). This helps retain moisture and adds extra protection against extreme drops in temperature, minimizing planting stress. Leaf mulch is a great benefit: you can use it to insulate the entire perennial garden, including mature plants. It breaks down naturally and can be easily removed or turned back into the perennial garden next spring.

A quick pass with the mower is a great way to shred fallen leaves, which add nutrients to the lawn.

Save the seeds of annuals such as snapdragons, cleome, and sunflowers to replant next spring—you'll get a plant you know you love at the best possible price.

 **Fall** Flower Garden

Dividing a perennial is easiest if you can find a natural division (*top*). Press a sharp spade into this division and cut the root ball (*bottom*).

*Get Growing*

Carefully remove and replant the section (*top*), then refill the original area with good soil (*bottom*).

## Planting Trees & Shrubs

Take advantage of the deep discounts on trees and shrubs in the fall. Just keep these planting tips in mind:

* Buy good-quality plants, free of damage and disease.
* Most deciduous trees can be planted from late summer until about three weeks before hard frost. The exceptions are poplar, willow, ash, elm, and birch, which are best planted in the spring to increase their chances of surviving their first winter.
* Evergreens are also best planted a few weeks before hard frost so the roots can get established and retain moisture before winter.
* Water well at planting time and again before the ground freezes to minimize the damage of winter drying.
* Use a transplant fertilizer, starter fertilizer, or bone meal to reduce transplant shock.
* Protect the bases of new trees from animal damage by using plastic collars or tree wrap.

## Winterizing Your Roses

If you have encouraged thick stems on your roses by fertilizing throughout the growing season, your plants will be able to store nutrients well. If you have watered them deeply, those long, deep roots will be strong enough to survive a freezing winter. If you've kept your roses free of insects and disease, they're as healthy and hearty as can be. But even then, many rose varieties (such as hybrid teas and floribunda) will need a little more TLC to get through the winter.

The purpose of winterizing roses is to protect the crown and roots. Roses can withstand the cold temperatures of winter: it is the alternating warm spells and cold snaps that do the damage. That's why roses need protection when the nights are freezing, even if the daytime temperatures are comfortable:

* Let the final blooms remain on the plant to turn to "hips," the berry-like fruit that roses produce after they finish flowering. This lets the plant know that the growing season is coming to an end.
* Clean up any diseased or decaying debris from the base of the plant that could provide homes for overwintering insects and disease.
* Continue to water deeply during the fall to provide moisture to see the plant through the winter months.
* After the first frost, prune to a height of 30 cm (12 inches), removing any canes thinner than a pencil, any that grow inwards, and any that are dead or diseased. Then cover the base of the plant with clean compost, leaves, or straw to protect the crown and roots. Hold this covering down with a layer of soil from another part of the garden, wire mesh, wood, or a Styrofoam rose collar.
* Standard (tree) roses can be very difficult to overwinter—that's why I don't recommend planting them. If you do have one, wrap the plant completely with burlap, being careful not to break the branches, and fully cover the base with straw or soil. If your standard rose is in a container, simply move the plant, pot and all, to a protected area like a garage or garden shed.

Winterizing roses means protecting them from the freeze-thaw cycle. Clear the area around the plant of any debris (*facing page*) and prune the canes back to about 30 cm (12 inches) after the first frost (*top*). Mulch heavily with compost, leaves, or straw to protect the crown and roots (*bottom*).

Pruning large deciduous trees is no easy task, and doing it improperly can result in property damage or serious injury. I strongly urge you to call an insured certified arborist to handle this job. A mature tree is a cherished and beautiful thing, and hiring a professional to look after it is money well spent.

# Pruning

Late fall and even early winter are good times to make an appointment with the horticultural hairdresser. Why? Because the leaves are gone, you have a better view of what you need to prune and the clean-up will be easier. The tree itself is also dormant at this time (so you're not stressing it while it's actively growing), and insects and disease are less prevalent and therefore less likely to invade the wounds.

How do you know if your tree needs a haircut? Look for the following:

* Branches are rubbing against the house or other trees.
* Branches are dead, storm-damaged, or diseased.
* Branches are growing toward the centre or rubbing other branches.
* Branches may interfere with power lines if they are laden with snow.
* Thinning out branches will improve air circulation and light.
* You want to improve the shape or reduce the height.

Here's what you need to remember about fall pruning:

* Prune most deciduous trees, shrubs, and fruit trees during dormancy: from late fall to early spring.
* The exceptions are birch and maple trees, which should be pruned in midsummer, when the leaves are out fully. (Otherwise, they will bleed sap.)
* Prune elms between October and March to prevent the spread of Dutch elm disease.
* When in doubt, take off less, not more: over-pruning in fall will reduce winter hardiness.
* Oak and elm pruning wounds should be sealed with Tanglefoot paste (available at the garden centre) to protect against insects. Note that this isn't the same as pruning paste, which I don't recommend.

# Creating Year-Round Interest

If you planned and planted your garden in the spring, your mind was probably filled with thoughts of lush green foliage and colourful blooms. Though many gardeners give little thought to how their landscape will look when summer is over, fall is an amazing time—it's the fireworks display at the closing ceremonies of another growing season! And even winter brings an opportunity to create some architectural interest in the garden.

If you love fall colours as much as I do, there's still time to make a spot for these plants in your landscape. You may not enjoy their full display this season, but next year they will shine:

### Sugar maple
(*Acer saccharum*)
The familiar shade tree that turns brilliant orange to red in the fall. This eastern North American native grows up to 20 m (65 feet) tall.

### Downy serviceberry
(*Amelanchier arborea*)
Leaves turn from yellow to red in the fall and

To maintain all-season interest, plant evergreens among perennials that will die back.

*Get Growing*

birds enjoy its fruit. (As a bonus, it has fragrant white flowers in spring.) Another Canadian native tree, it thrives in sun to partial shade and reaches up to 5 m (16 feet) in height.

### 'Limelight' hydrangea

(*Hydrangea paniculata* 'Limelight')
Sturdy stems with exquisite lime-green, trumpet-shaped flowers that blush to a deep pink in the fall. Plant it in sun to partial shade; it grows up to 2.5 m (8 feet) high.

### Virginia creeper

(*Parthenocissus quinquefolia*)
A grow-anywhere, cover-anything deciduous vine that turns red in autumn. It's very easy to grow in full sun to partial shade.

### Nannyberry

(*Viburnum lentago*)
Leathery, dark-green foliage turns purplish red in the fall, and in September it bears blue-black fruits that birds love. Tolerant of full sun to partial shade, it reaches up to 4 m (13 feet).

When you do your fall planting—or as you make notes for next year—plan ahead to add some winter interest too.

When designing any garden, I always try to include evergreens, which offer colour and substance all year long. They can shelter your home from cold winds and provide protection for birds. Evergreens trained into topiaries, spirals, and pom-poms create character for entrances. And they're the best place to hang your Christmas lights!

My only warning is that some evergreens can grow very big. That little blue spruce you planted this year may one day take up your entire yard or block your entranceway. Always consider the mature height when planting any tree or shrub. Smaller, slower-growing evergreens include yews, upright junipers, dwarf Alberta spruce, pyramidal cedars, and hemlock.

During one of your fall forays to the garden centre, you may want to pick up a statue or other garden structure. A properly placed statue surrounded by snow on a crisp winter's morning adds character to your garden. Arbours, pergolas, small fences, and gates add structure during a time when height and flow disappear with the snow.

Wind chill may be unpleasant for us, but fall and winter breezes captured by plants create movement and sound in the garden. That's one of the best reasons to plant ornamental grasses. The brown, tired foliage of Japanese silver grass swaying in the winds of old-man winter is a comforting sight, especially from the window of your home as you sit by the fire.

Any time you select trees and shrubs for the garden, keep in mind what their appearance will be in winter, when the leaves have dropped. The stems of corkscrew hazel, weeping birch, and pagoda dogwood provide an almost architectural interest. Red twig dogwood adds sprigs of spiky colour that pop out of snowbanks. They're also great to use alongside evergreen boughs in an urn placed near the entrance to your home.

Great choices for fall colour: sugar maple (*top left*), serviceberry (*top right*), 'Limelight' hydrangea (*bottom left*), Virginia creeper (*bottom right*).

*Get Growing*

Ornamental grasses continue looking great all year, even in winter when they tower and sway above the snow.

# Welcoming Birds into Your Garden

Birds add colour, sound, and movement to the garden during a time when we are in desperate need of all three. You can attract birds by planting trees, shrubs, and perennials that provide food and shelter during the winter months—any plant that produces berries or seed heads will do the trick. But if you really want action, put out a bird feeder.

There are many varieties of birdseed, and several varieties are marked "garden friendly," meaning they won't germinate in your garden. You can attract specific types of birds by selecting the right seed:

| Seed | Birds that like it |
| --- | --- |
| Black oil sunflower | Most birds—and squirrels too |
| Safflower | Cardinals, doves, chickadees, sparrows |
| White millet | Cardinals, doves, towhees, sparrows, juncos, blackbirds |
| Peanuts | Blue jays, crows, woodpeckers, chickadees |
| Cracked corn | Ducks, geese, crows—but also deer, squirrels, and more! |
| Thistle (nyjer) | Finches, pine siskins, redpolls |
| Golden millet, red millet, flax | These are just filler—don't buy mixes that contain them |

If birds are not coming to your feeder, you've probably placed it in an exposed area. Birds are fearful: they like to come to your feeder, pick a few seeds, and then fly quickly away for cover. So the best place to position a feeder is close to an evergreen tree. But not too close—keep it about 2 or 3 metres (7 to 10 feet) from the tree or you'll have squirrels jumping into the birds' feeding station.

## Bringing Tender Plants Indoors

If you have indoor plants that have been outside all summer, patio plants you want to save for next year, herbs that will grow inside, or annuals you wish to overwinter, move them in before the first frost. Here are some tips:

* Give your plants the once over for any little creatures that may move inside with them. Rinsing them off with a good spray of the hose is a good idea. Treat plants for aphids, spiders, ants, or any other insects you notice.

* Provide proper containers for any plants you are digging out of the garden. Be sure the pot has proper drainage and is large enough for the roots. Do not use soil from your garden, as it can carry diseases and pests: buy potting soil for all indoor plants.

* Cut back plants lightly when you move them indoors. This will encourage new growth and help the plant adjust to life indoors.

* Your plants will need to be acclimatized to the indoors. You can do this by keeping them in

To bring a tender plant indoors for the winter, dig it out of the ground, place it in a clean container of potting soil, and spray with insecticidal soap to prevent bringing insects indoors.

a shady location prior to moving them inside or by bringing them in for a few hours each day. (A super-sunny window inside in fall/winter is about equivalent in light levels to a shady spot outside.)

* Be sure you have a good indoor location: a bright, sunny spot is usually a requirement for anything that has been outside.

* The air inside your home is drier than out-doors, especially when you're running the furnace. Some plants, such as ferns, need additional humidity. A humidifier is ideal, but an occasional misting will also help. You can also place plants near the window in a well-lit bathroom—they'll love the high humidity when you run the shower.

* Place your plants out of reach of children and animals, as some can be toxic—the plants, that is!

* Make sure the leaves of your plants do not touch the windows. They can cook on the glass on sunny days and freeze on cold winter nights.

* Water indoor plants deeply and infrequently. Do not fertilize them, as this is not an active growing time for plants.

Cutting soft-stemmed perennials back in the fall makes the garden look neat and tidy. It will also save you a job next spring, when you'll be busy with a host of other garden tasks.

# Getting Ready for Winter

Some important tasks need to be completed in the fall in order to make sure your garden is ready to face the wrath of winter.

As I mentioned in the last chapter, you don't want to fertilize your shrubs, roses, and trees after midsummer—this would promote new growth that would be too tender to handle winter temperatures and wind. Likewise, stop pruning, especially evergreens. Pruning also promotes new growth, which is not what you want when you're heading into winter. Try to make sure your evergreen shrubs and trees get an extra deep watering before the hard winter sets in. This will help them retain moisture.

As the season winds down, start preparing your perennial garden. As each plant finishes blooming and begins to turn brown, cut it back to about 10 to 12 cm (4 to 5 inches) above the ground. Snow will gather in the remaining stems, offering a little protection and leaving a natural marker for next spring. Cutting back your perennials now also gives your garden a tidier appearance during the long winter months and reduces the amount of work you will have in the busy spring season. I do like to leave some perennials standing (such as purple coneflower and black-eyed Susan) to provide food for birds. They also provide some winter interest in the garden, as do ornamental grasses.

Winter weather can do all kinds of damage to your garden, but not in the way many people think. The freezing temperatures that keep you indoors rarely harm perennials, trees, and shrubs: most plants are dormant during winter, and they're actually more sensitive to the hot, dry, and stressful conditions of summer. Winter damage usually comes from four main culprits:

## Heavy snow

I remember coming home late one night in October and finding my cedars bent over from a freak early snowstorm. I did exactly what you should do in these circumstances: I shook the snow off. An early blast of heavy, wet snow like this can be really damaging, as trees and shrubs have not had time to allow cold temperatures to firm up their stems. Any accumulation on the branches and stems can cause them to bend and break.

To prevent damage from heavy snow, tie pyramidal evergreens with twine. (You don't need to do this for spreading evergreens—only those tall enough to be affected by snow loads.) If the tree is not too tall, I find it easiest to tie the twine on a strong bottom branch and then slowly spiral the twine around the tree all the way to the top. The twine bunches the branches together, so the tree is "closed up" like a furled umbrella.

Warmer days in late winter threaten garden beds that are under roof lines, as snow can slide off the roof and onto your prized plants. I've seen a lot of plants damaged in this way. If it's a problem on your property, use small A-frame structures to shelter your plants. At the same time, you should allow some snow to accumulate: snow is good for your plants, as it insulates them against extreme drops in temperature and provides an early dose of moisture when it melts in the spring.

If your evergreens are vulnerable to damage from heavy snow, wind twine around them in the fall.

Heavy, compacted snow can be damaging to garden beds near your driveway: when you shovel, avoid piling snow onto flowering shrubs and small evergreen hedges.

## Winter burn

You know how your lips crack and your skin becomes dry in winter? Dry, cold air can also suck the moisture from the needles of evergreens, causing winter burn, which turns them brown. To prevent this, restrict the amount of light the plant gets and protect it against wind. Burlap wrap does both. My favourite technique is to use burlap screens, as they still allow for airflow and some snow load. For evergreens located close to roads, driveways, and walkways, burlap also reduces salt-spray damage. You can set up burlap protection in late fall—after there have been several frosts and the garden has started to die back but before the ground freezes.

Strong, mature evergreens don't usually need winter protection. The ones most likely to need help are those that face northwest, those planted in a windy area, or those growing near a white wall—the sun will dry these out the most quickly. Smaller or newer evergreens also need some protection. I suggest building a frame around the plant and erecting a burlap screen:

1. Surround the tree or shrub with four wooden posts measuring about 20 cm (8 inches) taller than the plant and positioned about 20 cm (8 inches) away. Pound the posts into the ground using a wooden mallet. (Some evergreens, such as hedges along a roadway, need protection from only one side, so two posts may be enough.)

2. With a staple gun, attach one end of the burlap to one of the stakes. You may need to fold the burlap a couple of times before stapling it, so it doesn't tear away from the stake. Then unroll the burlap around the outside of the frame, stapling it to each pole where necessary as you go.

3. Leave the top open to allow snow to accumulate and insulate your prized plant.

Broadleaf evergreens such as rhododendrons benefit from burlap, too, and you can provide further protection from winter burn by applying an antidesiccant such as Wilt-Pruf. This product helps seal the moisture in, providing an additional level of insurance. Wilt-Pruf should be applied when cooler weather has set in, but for best results, use it on a day when temperatures are above freezing.

### Frankie's Tip

We're all aware of the damaging effects road salt can have on our pant legs and on the paint jobs on our cars, but many forget that salt accumulation on foliage and soil can be damaging— even life threatening—to plants in our landscape. Salt does the most harm in late winter, when plants are emerging out of dormancy. Where possible, I recommend using sand and plant-friendly ice melters, which are now widely available.

2047
9.0327-74

GROWN IN CANADA
CULTIVÉ AU CANADA

Shrubs that get a lot of exposure to winter wind can benefit from a burlap screen. Hammer wooden posts around the plant (*left*) and use a staple gun to attach the burlap (*right top*). Leave the top of the screen open to allow snow to collect around the base (*right bottom*) and allow air flow.

*Get Growing*

## Wildlife damage

I live on a 6,000 square metre (1.5-acre) wooded lot, so my property is regularly visited by anything that makes the forest its home. Winter can be a very hungry time for wildlife, as snow covers many food sources and plants are dormant. The result is that rabbits, deer, and rodents turn to our gardens for survival. In my experience, wildlife consider fruit trees, euonymus, and Japanese maples to be the most desirable.

You can do a couple of things to keep animals from tearing up your garden. Skoot is a product that you can apply to stems and branches of trees and shrubs when they're in dormancy. Skoot isn't toxic to animals; it's simply a repellent. It tastes awful (and smells pretty bad too) so animals may take one bite but never another.

Wrapping the trunks of young fruit trees with plastic collars can also prevent damage. Wrap as high up as you can: as the snow piles up, rabbits and mice will be able to reach higher on the trunk.

## Frost heaving

As you walk through your garden in winter, you may also notice that one or more of your newly planted specimens has popped out of the ground. The freezing and thawing of winter can cause new plants to move up and down and can sometimes even push them out of their planting holes. If the ground is soft enough, replant anything that has been heaved out by frost. If that's not an option, cover the root ball with a few bags of soil for insulation. If you have the space, keep an extra bag or two of soil handy for just this purpose.

Plastic collars protect young trees from being gnawed by hungry animals in winter.

**Fall** Flower Garden

If you store your tools with soil still clinging to them, you're inviting rust. Give them a scrape with a wire brush before stashing them for the winter.

*Get Growing*

## Shutting Down for the Season

We all know that water expands when it freezes. If you forgot that little fact from science class, it will all come back to you if you ever have a pipe burst in winter. Believe me, I speak from experience!

Before winter weather sets in, make sure you shut off the water supply to your outdoor taps. If you have an underground sprinkler system, you will also need to blow out the pipes with an air compressor. Drain your garden hoses, too, and store them in a shed or in the garage.

Any clay or stone planters need to be emptied, turned over, covered with a tarp, or placed in the garage for the winter. If you leave them upright and full of soil, they'll likely crack because of the expansion of freezing water in the soil. The same will happen if snow lands on the planters, melts, and then freezes. Take the same precautions with bird baths, fountains made of concrete, or any other garden structure that can allow water to pool.

If you have a water garden, the pump cannot be left to freeze and you can't allow it to dry out during winter, as this will shrink the gaskets. Pumps are best stored indoors in a bucket of water.

In addition to protecting your plants over the winter, you should also take care of your gardening products:

* Granular fertilizers must be kept dry and protected from repeated freezing and thawing. Ideally, keep them in a basement or an insulated garage.

* Liquid fertilizers must be stored indoors, as freezing will harm them.

* Liquid chemical and non-chemical herbicides and pest controls have a shelf life of more than one growing season, but they cannot be frozen and should be stored indoors. Make sure you keep them on a high shelf away from children.

* Corn gluten can be stored in a dry location like a garage, even if it dips below freezing. However, remember that this product is made from corn and will attract rats and mice, especially during winter. Keep it in a hard plastic pail with a tight-fitting lid.

As the growing winds down, take some time to do an inventory of your garden tools. Start by asking your friends and neighbours to return what they borrowed—when they're not using them, they're more likely to hand them over!

Garden tools are a big investment and taking a little time to remove dirt from spades and rakes with a wire brush will prevent rust and make your tools last longer. Wiping pruning shears with vegetable oil will lubricate them and improve their lifespan. When storing spades and shovels for the season, stick them into a pail of sand. Better yet, add a litre (a quart, or about a quarter gallon) of mineral oil to 20 litres (20 quarts, or about 5 gallons) of sand. The mixture will help to clean your tools and preserve their life.

# VEGETABLE GARDEN

**Your fall vegetable garden checklist:**

✔ Learn to recognize when your vegetables are ready to harvest.

✔ Pick tomatoes if there's a threat of frost and let them ripen off the vine.

✔ Remove and compost vegetable plants after they've finished producing.

✔ Plant a crop of green manure to enrich the soil for spring.

✔ Protect perennial crops such as strawberries, asparagus, and rhubarb to ensure healthy production next year.

✔ Plant garlic to harvest next fall.

✔ Store your fall harvest of root vegetables in a cool, dry place so you can enjoy them for weeks.

✔ Take note of what worked and what didn't in your vegetable garden this year and make plans to improve next season.

## Knowing When to Harvest

I'm Italian, so for me fall means roasting peppers, preparing tomatoes for sauce, and pickling eggplant! Knowing when to harvest these vegetables is important, and it can be tricky to determine the right time. Here are my tips, in approximate order of when they're ready:

Pick cucumbers when they are firm and dark green. Slicing cucumbers are ready when they are 15 to 20 cm (6 to 8 inches) long. Pickling cukes should be about 5 cm (2 inches) for sweet pickles. Varieties used for dills should be about 10 to 15 cm (4 to 6 inches). Process them immediately if you want crunchy pickles: if stored too long, they become soft.

Broccoli should be cut when the clusters are tight and green—before they separate and begin to flower. Cut early in the morning to avoid wilting. Do not remove the whole plant: cut above a place where the plant branches out. Then you may get a second, smaller crop.

Cut cauliflower when the heads are tight and white—before they turn yellow. Cut early in the day when the sugars are high in the stem.

Peppers can be picked at any time after they've reached full size. You can pick red bell peppers when they're still green, although they'll be much sweeter when they change to red. Just make sure you pick them before the first frost. Peppers will have a longer shelf life if a bit of stem is left on.

Tomatoes are ready to pick when they have a full, even colour. Don't let them get too big or they will split or crack. Use a sharp knife or clippers when picking tomatoes, leaving a bit of stem to help retain flavour. Never pull them off the vine, as you could damage the plant. If there is a frost warning before your tomatoes are ripe, pick them anyway and bring them indoors to ripen.

You can tell when potatoes are ready to harvest at this time of year because the vines will die back and turn brown. (New potatoes are dug earlier, as soon as the flower has faded.)

After digging, be sure to keep potatoes in a cool, dark, and dry spot. The sun causes them to develop a green skin that is actually toxic.

Eggplants are ready for picking when they are 15 to 20 cm (6 to 8 inches) long and are firm and shiny.

Corn is ready when the silks turn darker than their original colour. Open the cob slightly in one place and check by squeezing a kernel: if a milky fluid squirts out, it's ready. For the best flavour, pick corn right before you're ready to eat it: the longer it is left, the more the sugars will turn to starch.

Ask any farmer growing onions and they'll tell you that when the tops fall over and turn yellow, it's harvest time.

Garlic is ready to harvest when the lower half of the leaves are brown. Harvest before the wrapper on the bulb begins to break down. Take garlic out of the sun immediately to keep the flavour.

You know cantaloupes are ready when the skin has a netted texture. At this point the cantaloupe will separate from the vine with a gentle tug.

Watermelon does not ripen further after picking, so be sure yours is ready before you harvest it. Look at the vine: if it is withered close to the melon, it's probably time. If the melon has a white underbelly and a dull skin and if it sounds hollow when knocked on, it's ready.

Pumpkins that have turned from green to orange are ready to pick when the vine withers and the pumpkin has reached a good size. Leave a 10 cm (4 inch) stem on the pumpkin to keep it from rotting—and besides, a pumpkin just looks better with a stem.

As with pumpkins, squash is ready when the vine has withered. Check to be sure the shell and stem are hard: that's an indication that your squash will not rot.

Cut cabbage when heads feel very hard: if they're still soft when you squeeze them, they're not mature. Again, harvest them early on a cloudy day to avoid wilting and to retain flavour.

Although this cabbage might look a little chewed, it's totally fine. Just harvest, peel back any damaged leaves, and enjoy!

# Ripening Tomatoes Off the Vine

Tomatoes turn red for exactly the same reason that leaves change colour. A green tomato is full of chlorophyll, and when this chlorophyll breaks down, the natural pigments (carotenoids) shine through and turn the tomato red!

Ethylene gas given off by other fruits and vegetables promotes the breakdown of chlorophyll, so placing a ripe apple or banana with green tomatoes speeds up the ripening process. But keep an eye on things—sometimes this happens too quickly, causing the tomatoes to rot.

If you have just a few tomatoes, place them on a windowsill or in a brown paper bag to speed up the ripening process.

More than a few? Place them in layers in a large cardboard box, separating the layers with newspapers, and add an apple or banana to speed the process.

Entire crop of tomatoes? Spread newspapers on the garage floor, lay out the green tomatoes, and cover with more newspapers.

Want a method that's fast, easy, and fun? Pull the tomato plant out of the garden, root and all, hang it upside down, and watch the green tomatoes turn red!

Tomatoes picked early will ripen in a sunny window. Placing a ripe tomato nearby releases ethylene, which will help the others ripen more quickly.

Swiss chard is a great, hardy vegetable that will keep growing all season—as long as you keep harvesting it.

# Laying the Groundwork for Next Year

The harvest is complete, but we can't leave the vegetable garden just yet. The end of one growing season is also the beginning of the next one!

As the last of the season's vegetables are harvested, the plants can be pulled out and left to decompose right there in the garden. Some of them can go in the composter, but anything that is diseased should be thrown out with the yard waste or burned. As the vegetation breaks down, it replenishes the soil with the nutrients lost during the growing season.

If your composter has been cooking all summer, take time now to spread finished compost over the garden area and dig it into the soil. (This job can be left until spring, but since that's such a busy time, I find it easier to do it in the fall.) Over the winter, the alternating freezing and thawing temperatures will break down the organic matter, leaving the soil nutrient-rich and fertile. It may also prevent perennial weeds from overwintering.

Another organic method of adding nutrients to the soil is planting a cover crop—also known as green manure. Here's how it works: as you remove vegetable plants in late summer and early fall, work the ground and seed it with a fast-germinating crop that's high in nitrogen and other nutrients. Grass crops or legumes are the most commonly used, including ryegrass, buckwheat, oats, barley, soya beans, or clover. (These are hard to find at the garden centre—you may need to go to a farm supply store.) In the early spring, you dig the crop back into the soil, where it breaks down quickly. As well as being useful for adding organic matter to your soil, green manure serves as a mulch to discourage weeds from growing and to hold the moisture in the soil. It also prevents erosion and the leaching of nutrients from the soil by rain and snow.

# Tending Perennial Crops

While most of the plants in your vegetable garden need to be planted every year, a few of them are perennial and need some extra attention to prepare for winter:

Strawberry plants have already set their buds for the next growing season, and these need to be protected when the plant goes dormant. In addition, the freezing and thawing temperatures of winter can actually heave the plant right out of the ground. A clean mulch of straw, corn husks, bark chips, or well-composted manure will protect your strawberry plants. Cover with 5 to 8 cm (2 to 3 inches) of mulch in late fall. (Covering them too early, before hard frost, may cause your plants to rot.) Remember to uncover them early in the spring!

After a few killing frosts, cut your asparagus foliage down to the ground to keep overwintering insects away. Spread some manure or mulch (the same stuff you used for your strawberries) over the asparagus patch to fertilize and protect the plants at the same time.

Rhubarb needs cold temperatures to remain productive for the next growing season, and it is a plant that does fine without protection. However, in order to get things growing

Remove vegetable plants from the garden as soon as they're spent. Keeping the garden clean and airy in the fall can help prevent disease and will encourage healthy crops next year.

*Get Growing*

Mulching strawberry plants heavily after hard frost will protect next year's buds. Just remember to uncover them early in spring.

 **Fall** Vegetable Garden

earlier in the spring, you may want to add manure and then mulch the plant after hard frost.

Finally, there's one crop that's actually planted in early fall: garlic. Ideally, garlic should be planted early enough in the fall for the roots to develop, but not so early that sprouts break through the soil. Follow these garlic-growing tips:

* Purchase garlic bulbs at the same time that you purchase your spring-flowering bulbs.
* Plant garlic in well-drained soil that is rich in organic matter.
* Before planting, separate the bulbs into cloves. (This is called "cracking.")
* For optimum results, plant only the largest cloves: use the smaller ones for cooking, as they probably won't develop into large bulbs.
* Plant cloves pointed side up, in rows 20 cm (8 inches) apart and about 5 cm (2 inches) deep.
* Mulch for winter protection.

## Storing Your Fall Harvest

When you look out the window at the blanket of snow covering your garden, fresh vegetables may seem like a distant memory. However, you can continue to enjoy your harvest during the winter as long as you store your vegetables properly.

Root crops such as potatoes, onions, carrots, and beets—and even some cabbages—will still be great for eating. If they're properly stored in a traditional fruit cellar, where they're kept cool, dark, and dry, root vegetables can last for

weeks. Check on your stored vegetables occasionally, removing any rotten ones immediately.

Other than that, there isn't much to do after your harvest is complete. You can satisfy your gardening urge by planning next season's crop: make notes on the vegetables you had too many of, those you were lacking, those you didn't eat, and those that just didn't grow well. Next year you'll get it all right!

Garlic is the only crop that's planted in fall. Separate the cloves into buds and plant them about 5 cm (2 inches) deep.

The fall harvest is the most rewarding time of year! Some crops, such as onions and even some cabbages, will keep for weeks if properly stored in a cool, dark place.

 **Fall** Vegetable Garden

Full of peonies and hostas in the summer,
this garden becomes a wasteland in winter.
Make sure to consider year-round interest when you plant,
or invest in yardwaste bins to add colour (kidding)!

# LAWN

## Your fall lawn checklist:

- ✔ Seed or lay sod for a new lawn if necessary.
- ✔ Dethatch, aerate, top-dress, and overseed your lawn to promote vibrant growth.
- ✔ Give the lawn one last mowing before the snow arrives.
- ✔ Apply a lawn fertilizer formulated for fall, which will help the grass develop strong roots.
- ✔ If you have a heavy load of fallen leaves, rake as many as you can.
- ✔ Have your lawn mower serviced.
- ✔ If a lot of snow arrives before the fall is over, remove compacted mounds of the white stuff in order to prevent snow mould.

The arrival of cooler days and more frequent rain will have your lawn turning green again as it bounces out of the dormancy that summer drought may have caused. Grass loves cool weather, and as we've said, it thrives when it gets a weekly watering of at least 2.5 cm (1 inch). (If Mother Nature isn't providing an inch of water per week, keep watering until the first hard frost.)

Late summer and fall are perfect times to put in a new lawn: the heavy morning dew keeps things cool and moist, and these are just the right conditions for the germination of grass seed. Just follow the steps in the Early Spring chapter (see "Starting a Lawn from Scratch," page 15).

# Helping Your Lawn Flourish

Alittle sweat equity in fall goes a long way toward helping your lawn flourish next season. Many of the steps are similar to the ones we discussed in the Early Spring chapter, but here's a refresher:

### Rake to dethatch

Lawns left to overwinter with thick layers of thatch are more likely to pick up fungal diseases. If you dig up a plug of grass and find the brown, matted part is 1 cm (1/2 inch) thick or more, it's time to dethatch. After completing the job and picking up all the debris, your lawn will probably look terrible for a short time—but don't worry, it will bounce back. This is a cool-weather job because of the stress it puts on your lawn.

### Aerate

If your property has clay-based soil or your lawn gets a lot of foot traffic, it will benefit from being aerated now as well as in early spring. Make sure you do this before fertilizing.

### Add a layer of top dressing

Top dressing is the process of adding a thin layer of nutrient-rich soil. If the soil under your lawn is poor, top dressing will provide new soil to encourage more root growth, retain moisture, and receive nutrients. The result will be a thicker, more drought-tolerant lawn that is able to crowd out the growth of new weeds. Top dressing also fills out any bumps or ridges formed by the lawn mower over the summer.

### Overseed

With the soil refreshed and clear of thatch and the lawn filled with holes left by aerating, grass seed has the ideal conditions to germinate. To thicken your lawn, broadcast seed and lightly rake the top dressing. Keep the area moist until the seed germinates.

About three weeks after following these steps, your lawn should be looking better than ever. Continue with regular lawn maintenance throughout the fall: weeding, watering, and cutting. Set your mower's height at about 5 cm (2 inches) to keep the grass from bending with the weight of the snow and to discourage the growth of fungal diseases such as snow mould.

Never toss diseased leaves in the composter: put them on the curb with the rest of your fall yard waste.

Dethatching your lawn in fall will prevent overwintering diseases and give the grass a head start next spring.

*Get Growing*

## Last-Minute Care and Feeding

**Y**our lawn is like a bear preparing to hibernate, and the happiest and healthiest bears are those that are well fed. Before the snow flies, fertilize your lawn with a product specially formulated for this season. Fall fertilizers have higher phosphorus levels (the middle number) to encourage healthier roots and higher potassium levels (the third number) to offer winter protection.

Of course, it wouldn't be fall if your lawn wasn't eventually covered in leaves, and these can be a natural fertilizer. If it's just a light layer—and there are no signs of disease on the leaves—you can simply shred them with the lawn mower to provide nutrients. If you've let the lawn get ragged, you should give it a quick mow before the snow arrives. Make sure the grass is no more than 5 to 8 cm (2 to 3 inches) high: any taller and the blades of grass will bend over with the weight of snow, smothering the lawn.

If you've got a heavy load of leaves, rake as many as you can. You can shred some and add them to the composter; use them for winter protection around perennials, shrubs, and trees; or lay them down as mulch to reduce weeds. (If you dig some of the shredded leaves into the garden now, they will be fully decomposed by spring, improving the drainage and fertility of the soil.) Remember, any leaves that show signs of disease should be put on the curb with your yard waste instead of into the garden or compost. This will minimize recurrence of diseases next season.

As in the garden, snow insulates and helps provide early-spring moisture in the lawn. But compacted snow can create snow mould. The damage won't be visible until spring, but winter is the time to prevent it. Snow mould usually appears where you pile snow after shovelling it from walkways and the driveway. Ideally, you should try not to pile it up, but let's face it: there are only so many places you can put the snow. What's more realistic is to wait for a mild, sunny day in late winter and spread the white stuff over a large area so it melts more quickly. I've found that spreading snow on the driveway speeds the process. Ironic, isn't it—you spent a whole season shovelling snow off the driveway, and now you're shovelling it back on!

**Congratulations—you've survived the growing season! I hope you enjoyed your journey from the first buds of early spring to the last falling leaf of autumn. As the snow begins to cover your lawn and garden, you may feel some separation anxiety. But the coming winter is really a good thing—like spouses, gardeners and plants need to spend a little time apart so they learn to appreciate each other!**

**Fall** Lawn

A light layer of leaves can just be shredded with the mower, but bigger piles need to be raked and removed. Use a sturdy fan rake to make this job easier.

**Fall** Lawn

Winter

# Rest and Reflection

In the Ontario town where I live, winter can be long and full of challenges: bitter cold and driving snow are hardly welcome guests. But snow is the first sign of the season, and soon trees, shrubs, and perennials are fully dormant. In the garden, ponds freeze over and birds are searching for leftover seed heads as a source of food. In winter, you can enjoy your garden by just looking out the window of your living room!

But the coldest season also offers some interesting opportunities for gardeners. I encourage you to take a positive, proactive approach to winter. Take the time to learn about new plants or techniques to try next year. Reflect on the year's gardening successes and blunders. Remember, a garden is always a work in progress, never a finished product.

Here are some suggestions for how to spend the snowy season. But we're taking it easy in winter, so these ideas are strictly optional—no checklists this time!

I can't stop thinking about gardening, even in winter! When the snow flies, I like to curl up indoors with a seed catalogue.

# Handling Gardening Withdrawal

I go through some intense periods of gardening withdrawal. So I find the best thing to do on a cold, dreary winter day is to pull out some photos and notes from the last gardening season. Looking at these allows me to reflect on my successes, correct my mistakes, and plan and budget for next year.

Winter also provides an opportunity to further your knowledge of gardening by reading books or even taking online courses offered by horticultural schools.

January and February are the months when many mail-order companies send out their seed catalogues. I love them: the photography is great, the prices are reasonable, and placing an order is just a phone call or web click away. But a few words of caution. First, the plants never look as good in my garden as they do in the pictures. Second, you'll need to make sure you have a suitable spot in your garden for that plant that looks so tempting. Finally, starting seeds indoors is time consuming—do you really want to do that? And trust me, purchasing during a period of garden withdrawal is never a good idea!

If you do decide to order seeds by mail, do some Internet research first: look for reviews about the integrity of the seed company and learn from the experience of gardeners who've grown some of the varieties you're looking at.

# Growing Indoor Plants

Looking for a way to experience gardening all winter? Start growing plants indoors. My favourite is amaryllis, one of the few plants that will bloom with huge flowers in the dead of winter. Amaryllis can be purchased as a bulb, in a kit with pot and soil included, or preplanted. Place the potted bulb in indirect light, keep it moist, and in a few weeks you'll be rewarded with a stunning bloom that will lift you out of the winter blahs.

Here are my other indoor favourites:

**ZZ plant** (*Zamioculcas zamiifolia*)
Easy to grow and has an exotic, tropical form that looks great on desks and tabletops.

**Snake plant, or mother-in-law's tongue** (*Sansevieria trifasciata*)
Tall, swordlike leaves will make you think of the 1970s, when it seemed like everyone had one of these bulletproof houseplants.

**Philodendron**
Grow well in low to medium light. In addition to looking great, they remove toxins from the air.

**Christmas cactus**
Amazingly long-lived and easy to care for, they're also one of a very small number of houseplants that blooms in winter.

**Spider plant** (*Chlorophytum*)
Fun for kids because they send out little "babies" that are easy to transplant.

Christmas cactus (*above*), ZZ plant (*facing page, top left*), snake plant (*facing page, top right*), amaryllis (*facing page, bottom left*), spider plant (*facing page, bottom right*)

*Get Growing*

## Frankie's Tip

*If you're thinking of continuing the great Canadian tradition of building a skating rink, you should know that it can be excessively stressful for your lawn: your grass is almost certainly going to suffer some damage. I suggest building your rink in an area that will not jeopardize the curb appeal of your home.*

7047
9.0327-74

GROWN IN CANADA
CULTIVÉ AU CANADA

⚠
PP

Even though indoor plants are green and appear healthy in winter, the minimal sunlight of this season means they are not actively growing, so they don't require fertilizer or frequent watering. I suggest holding off on fertilizing indoor plants from October through March.

Remember that the number 1 killer of indoor plants is overwatering—or, as I like to say, "killing with kindness." The best way to check whether indoor plants require watering is the trusty old finger-touch method: stick your finger about 2.5 cm (1 inch) into the soil. If it feels moist, don't water the plant. Only water if the soil is crusty and dry.

The best technique for watering small indoor plants—assuming they are in pots with drainage holes—is to put them in the sink. Fill the sink with about 5cm (2 inches) of water and place the potted plant directly in the water for an hour. Presto, the water will draw directly and evenly into the pot.

Besides overwatering, three other factors could threaten the well-being of your indoor plants:

### Windows

Ensure that your plants are getting enough sunlight but always place them far enough from windows that they're not touching the glass. Otherwise, the leaves will likely be damaged by winter's chill.

### Heat sources

Your plants may look great beside the TV, sound system, or fireplace, but those are the worst locations for them because they all give off heat. Plants like consistent temperatures. The best place for them is in a grouping on the floor away from heating vents or drafts or on a table away from anything that will alter the temperature.

### Humidity

Humidity is key for plants, and indoor air tends to be very dry in winter. The best thing for both you and your plants is a humidifier. If that's not practical, try placing plants on a pebble tray filled with water: this increases humidity as the water evaporates. Grouping plants together and giving them an occasional misting helps too.

## Pruning Fruit Trees

There is one outdoor gardening task you can do in winter. Fruit trees such as apple, pear, plum, and cherry are dormant, so pruning them now will minimize stress. Start by removing any inward-growing branches and weak growth. Then shape the tree for improved airflow, fruit production, and appearance.

Overwatering is the enemy of houseplants. Use the finger-touch method: water the plant only if the soil feels crusty and dry.

# Pruning a Fruit Tree

Pruning fruit trees is one of the few chores you need to perform in a garden in winter—but it doesn't need to be complicated. Here are the things to consider before you cut.

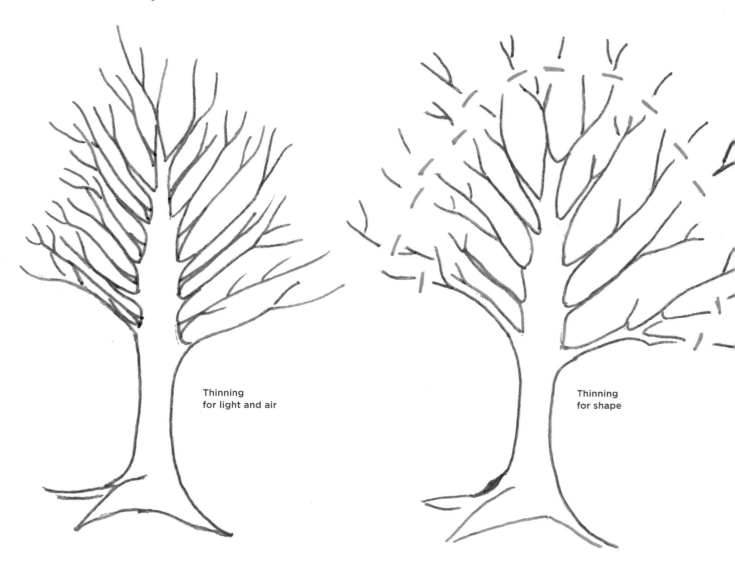

Thinning
for light and air

Thinning
for shape

There are two basic types of cuts: thinning cuts (*left*) don't reduce the overall size of a tree, but they create more space for air and light; heading cuts (*right*) reduce the size of the tree and alter its shape, invigorating the tree and spurring new growth.

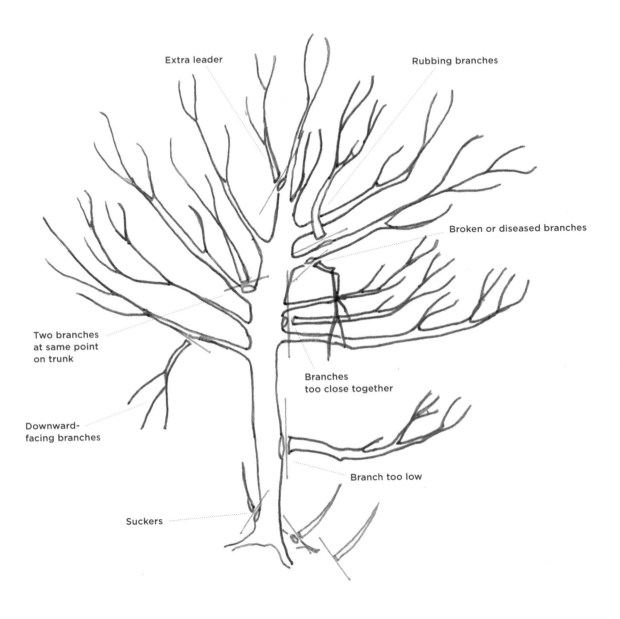

Extra leader

Rubbing branches

Broken or diseased branches

Two branches
at same point
on trunk

Branches
too close together

Downward-
facing branches

Branch too low

Suckers

When two branches emerge from the same point on the trunk, remove the weakest one. Cut away inward or downward-facing branches. Remove suckers growing at the base of the tree. If the tree has more than one leader (vertical branch at the top), leave only the straightest one. Cut away any branches that are rubbing against others. Discard broken or diseased branches. Thin out branches that are growing too close together. Remove large branches close to the ground.

The general rule of thumb for fruit trees is to prune them any time after they've lost all of their leaves and winter has firmly set in. This is known as the dormant stage.

There are two main types of cuts you can make when pruning a fruit tree. A thinning cut removes an entire shoot or branch, right back to a large lateral (horizontal or relatively horizontal) branch or the main trunk. This kind of cut does not promote vigorous new growth. In this case, you're just thinning out a tree to remove branches that don't look good. The other type of cut to use when pruning a fruit tree is a heading cut. This just shortens a branch, rather than removing it entirely. "Heading back" invigorates a fruit tree and encourages branching.

I enjoy winter—I really do like to take a break from gardening. But I think most gardeners feel the itch again by the end of January—once the holiday rush is forgotten and the new year is in full swing. By then I just can't wait to get back to the soil. I hope you'll feel the same way as next spring approaches. Having come this far, you'll be comfortable with the basics; the rest you'll learn through trial and error. You'll have many successes, but when you fail, just get back up and keep on blooming!

## Potted Christmas Trees

It sounds like a fantastic idea: buying a potted Christmas tree, keeping it indoors for the holidays, and then planting it outside afterwards. Unfortunately, the reality is not that simple. I'm really not a fan of bringing potted trees indoors. In my experience, they don't usually survive the ordeal. Bringing them inside will snap them out of dormancy, and putting them back outdoors will stress them and often cause them to die.

If you want to try your luck with a potted Christmas tree, the key is to have it indoors for the shortest amount of time possible—no more than a few days. I recommend bringing it inside on Christmas Eve, decorating it, enjoying it on Christmas morning, and then getting it back outdoors immediately thereafter.

If the ground is still workable, dig a hole and plant the tree immediately: evergreen survival rates jump when the root ball is placed in the ground. (If you plan ahead, you can dig the hole before freeze-up.) If it's not possible to replant the tree yet, place it in a sheltered, shady location where snow collects: that will provide additional insulation for the root ball.

*Get Growing*

# Acknowledgements

Wow, my first book—and let me tell you, a book is more work than you could ever imagine! *Get Growing!* would not have been possible without the help of a number of people.

I could never have completed the book without the love and support of my wife and best friend, Laurie. With two boys under three, Laurie had a challenging year, but she always gave me a warm smile when the book took me away from family responsibilities.

To my mother, Alyce; my father, Tony; and my sister Chaira: thank you for giving me the work ethic to get things done, to live with passion, and to believe in myself.

To the entire HarperCollins team: thank you for the opportunity and the positive experience it has been. Special thanks to Kate Cassaday for being a fantastic editor and now a wonderful friend.

To Dan Bortolotti, who guided me through the writing process: thank you for your patience and willingness to help make this a great gardening book.

To Shannon Ross, my partner in crime: your photography is beautiful, and you are a wonderful person to work with.

The help of my team of readers was invaluable: thanks to Norma Belfry, Val Cassaday, Alyce Ferragine, Dilys Halford, and Sonja Morgan.

I would also like to express my gratitude for the support, assistance, and suggestions I received from Beth Edney, Nicoletta Oppesdisano, Landscape Ontario, Bradford Greenhouses, Nature Mix Soils, and my friends and family at Breakfast Television.

Thank you as well to the Toronto Botanical Garden and to Chad and Cara Cole for allowing us to shoot in your gardens.

I'm grateful to the viewers of Citytv programs and the readers of my gardening articles in *Canadian Living*. I hope you have found inspiration through my Frankie Flowers philosophy of getting down and dirty!

Finally, to my brother Tony: you left this world in 1998, but your voice will live within me forever. Your short life has fuelled my desire to reach for the stars because I know that's where you're watching from.

**Frank Ferragine
aka Frankie Flowers**

Thanks to you, the reader, who have taken an interest and purchased this book of ours. May you learn a few new tricks and do so surrounded by beauty.

To be included in such a wonderful and fulfilling project has been certainly one of the new high points in my career. When I was first approached about this new challenge, I must admit I had no idea what lay in store but I have been pleasantly surprised every day of the process.

I owe sincere thanks to HarperCollins; my editor, Kate Cassaday; and, of course, Frankie for seeing my vision and including me in this project. It has been truly wonderful to work with such talented and motivated people. Every day they bring their best to bear and work with complement ary talents to achieve beautiful and compelling results. I consider myself more than fortunate to work with people like you. Frankie and Kate, you both define brilliance.

To Frankie's parents, Alyce and Tony, thanks for making a hard job much easier. Your excellent help, great lunches, and cold drinks helped keep the inspirational tap flowing.

I would also like to thank my own family for always being there. To my parents, Robert and Joanne, for bringing me up to respect and pursue the arts and for nurturing in me the skills that allowed me to do so. And to my wife, Robyn, who has always seen the best in what I do and who makes me remember why life is so sweet.

**Shannon J. Ross**

# Plant Index

| | Common name | Latin name | Light |
|---|---|---|---|
| | Ageratum | *Ageratum houstonianum* | Part sun |
| | Allium | *Allium azureum* | Full sun |
| | Alyssum (sweet alyssum) | *Alyssum maritimum* | Part sun to full sun |
| | Alyssum 'Mountain Gold' | *Alyssum montanum* | Full sun |
| | Amaranthus (love-lies-bleeding) | *Amaranthus caudatus* | Full sun |
| | Asiatic lily | *Lilium lancifolium* (plus others) | Full sun |

| | Common name | Latin name | Light |
|---|---|---|---|
| | Aster | *Aster* | Full sun |
| | Astilbe | *Astilbe* | Shade to part sun |
| | Azalea | *Azalea* | Shade to part sun |
| | Baby's breath | *Gypsophila paniculata* | Sun |
| | Bachelor's button (cornflower) | *Centaurea cyanus* | Full sun |
| | Barberry | *Berberis* | Full sun |
| | Basil | *Ocimum basilicum* | Full sun |

| | Common name | Latin name | Light |
|---|---|---|---|
| | Begonia | *Begonia semperflorens* | Sun or shade |
| | Birch | *Betula* | Full sun |
| | Black medic | *Medicago lupulina* | Part to full sun |
| | Black-eyed Susan | *Rudbeckia hirta* | Full sun |
| | Bleeding heart | *Dicentra* | Part shade to shade |
| | Blue fescue | *Festuca glauca* | Full sun |
| | Boston ivy | *Parthenocissus tricuspidata* | Full sun |

| | Common name | Latin name | Light |
|---|---|---|---|
| | Bougainvillea | *Bougainvillea* | Full sun |
| | Box elder | *Acer negundo* | Full sun |
| | Boxwood | *Buxus sempervirens* | Full sun |
| | Broadleaf plantain | *Plantago major* | Full sun |
| | Browallia | *Browallia* | Shade |
| | Bugleweed | *Ajuga reptans* | Shade |
| | Butterfly bush | *Buddleia davidii* | Full sun |

| | Common name | Latin name | Light |
|---|---|---|---|
| | Caladium | *Caladium* | Part sun |
| | Candytuft | *Iberis* | Full sun |
| | Canna lily | *Canna* | Full sun |
| | Canterbury bells | *Campanula medium* | Part sun |
| | Cedar | *Thuja occidentalis* | Part to full sun |
| | Chickweed | *Stellaria media* | Part shade |
| | Chives | *Allium schoenoprasum* | Full sun to part shade |

| | Common name | Latin name | Light |
|---|---|---|---|
| | Christmas cactus | *Schlumbergera* | Part sun |
| | Clematis | *Clematis* | Full to part sun |
| | Coleus | *Solenostemon* | Sun or shade (dependent on variety) |
| | Columbine | *Aquilegia* | Full to part sun |
| | Coneflower | *Echinacea* | Full sun |
| | Coral bells | *Heuchera* | Part shade |
| | Coreopsis | *Coreopsis* | Full sun |

| | Common name | Latin name | Light |
|---|---|---|---|
| | Corkscrew hazel | *Corylus avellana* 'Contorta' | Full to part sun |
| | Cosmos | *Cosmos bipinnatus* | Full sun |
| | Crabgrass | *Digitaria* | Full to part sun |
| | Creeping charlie | *Glechoma hederacea* | Part sun to shade |
| | Crocus | *Crocus* | Full to part sun |
| | Daffodil | *Narcissus* | Full to part sun |
| | Dahlia | *Dahlia* | Full sun |

| | Common name | Latin name | Light |
|---|---|---|---|
| | Daphne | *Daphne* | Full to part sun |
| | Day lily | *Hemerocallis* | Full to part sun |
| | Delphinium (larkspur) | *Delphinium* | Full to part sun |
| | Dianthus | *Dianthus* | Full sun |
| | Dogwood | *Cornus* | Full to part sun |
| | Downy serviceberry | *Amelanchier arborea* | Full to part sun |
| | Dracaena (spike) | *Cordyline indivisa* | Full sun |

| | Common name | Latin name | Light |
|---|---|---|---|
| | Dusty miller | *Senecio cineraria* | Full sun |
| | Elderberry (lace shrub) | *Sambucus canadensis laciniata* | Full to part sun |
| | English daisy | *Bellis perennis* | Full sun to part shade |
| | English Ivy | *Hedera helix* | Full to part sun |
| | Euonymous | *Euonymus fortunei* | Full to part sun |
| | False spirea | *Sorbaria sorbifolia* | Full sun to shade |
| | Fern (ostrich fern) | *Matteuccia struthiopteris* | Shade |

| | Common name | Latin name | Light |
|---|---|---|---|
| | Flowering almond | *Prunus triloba plena* | Full sun |
| | Forget-me-not | *Myosotis sylvatica* | Full sun to shade |
| | Forsythia | *Forsythia ovata* | Full sun |
| | Foxglove | *Digitalis* x *mertonensis* | Full sun to part shade |
| | Fritillaria (crown imperial) | *Fritillaria imperialis* | Full to part sun |
| | Fuchsia | *Fuchsia* | Full to part sun |
| | Geranium | *Pelargonium* | Full sun |

| | Common name | Latin name | Light |
|---|---|---|---|
| | Gladiolus | Gladiolus | Full Sun |
| | Hemlock | *Tsuga canadensis* | Full sun to shade |
| | Hibiscus—tropical | *Hibiscus rosa-sinensis* | Full sun |
| | Hollyhock | *Alcea rosea* | Full to part sun |
| | Hosta | *Hosta* | Part shade to shade |
| | Hyacinth | *Hyacinthus orientalis* | Full to part sun |
| | Hydrangea 'Limelight' | *Hydrangea paniculata* 'Limelight' | Full to part sun |

| | Common name | Latin name | Light |
|---|---|---|---|
| | Impatiens (busy lizzy) | *Impatiens walleriana* | Part shade to shade |
| | Iris—Siberian | *Iris sibirica* | Full to part sun |
| | Juniper | *Juniperus* | Full sun |
| | Lamb's ear | *Stachys byzantina* | Full to part sun |
| | Lamium (dead nettle) | *Lamium maculatum* | Part shade to shade |
| | Liatris | *Liatris spicata* | Full sun |
| | Lilac | *Syringa vulgaris* | Full sun |

| | Common name | Latin name | Light |
|---|---|---|---|
| | Lobelia | *Lobelia erinus* | Full sun to shade |
| | Locust | *Gleditsia* | Full to part sun |
| | Lupine | *Lupinus* | Full sun |
| | Magnolia | *Magnolia* x *loebneri* | Full to part sun |
| | Maple | *Acer* | Full sun |
| | Marigold | *Tagetes patula* | Full sun |
| | Morning glory | *Ipomoea nil* | Full to part sun |

| | Common name | Latin name | Light |
|---|---|---|---|
| | Mum | *Chrysanthemum sp* | Full to part sun |
| | Nannyberry | *Viburnum lentago* | Full sun |
| | Nasturtium | *Tropaeolum majus* | Full to part sun |
| | Nemesia | *Nemesia fruticans* | Full to part sun |
| | Nicotiana (tobacco plant) | *Nicotiana tabacum* | Full sun |
| | Oak | *Quercus* | Full sun |
| | Oleander | *Nerium oleander* | Full sun |

| | Common name | Latin name | Light |
|---|---|---|---|
| | Oregano | *Origanum vulgare* | Full to part sun |
| | Oriental poppy | *Papaver orientale* | Full to part sun |
| | Ornamental cabbage | *Brassica oleracea* | Full to part sun |
| | Ornamental grasses | Variety dependent | Variety dependent |
| | Ornamental kale | *Brassica oleracea* | Full to part sun |
| | Osteospermum (Cape daisy) | *Osteospermum* | Full sun |
| | Pansy | *Viola* | Full to part sun |

| | Common name | Latin name | Light |
|---|---|---|---|
| | Pansy—fall | *Viola* x *wittrockiana* | Full to part sun |
| | Parsley | *Petroselinum crispum* | Full to part sun |
| | Peony | *Paeonia* | Full sun |
| | Periwinkle | *Vinca minor* | Part shade to shade |
| | Petunia | *Petunia* x *hybrida* | Full sun |
| | Petunia 'Wave' | *Petunia* x *hybrida* 'Wave' | Full sun |
| | Philodendron | *Philodendron selloum* | Part sun |

| | Common name | Latin name | Light |
|---|---|---|---|
| | Phlox | *Phlox paniculata* | Full to part sun |
| | Pine | *Pinus* | Full sun |
| | Potentilla | *Potentilla fruticosa* | Full sun |
| | Primrose (primula) | *Primula* | Part shade |
| | Raspberries | *Rubus* | Full to part sun |
| | Rhododendron | *Rhododendron* | Part sun |
| | Rhubarb | *Rheum rhabarbarum* | Full sun |

| | Common name | Latin name | Light |
|---|---|---|---|
| | Rose | *Rosa* | Full sun |
| | Rose of Sharon | *Hibiscus syriacus* | Full sun |
| | Rosemary | *Rosmarinus officinalis* | Full sun |
| | Rudbeckia | *Rudbeckia fulgida* | Full sun |
| | Sage | *Salvia officinalis* | Full sun |
| | Salvia | *Veronica* | Full sun |
| | Scilla | *Scilla* | Full to part sun |

| | Common name | Latin name | Light |
|---|---|---|---|
| | Sedum | *Sedum* | Full sun |
| | Shasta daisy | *Leucanthemum* x *superbum* | Full to part sun |
| | Snake plant | *Sansevieria trifasciata* | Full to part sun |
| | Snapdragon | *Antirrhinum majus* | Full to part sun |
| | Spider plant | *Chlorophytum comosum* | Full sun to shade |
| | Spirea | *Spiraea* x *bumalda* | Full to part sun |
| | Spruce | *Picea* | Full sun |

| | Common name | Latin name | Light |
|---|---|---|---|
| | Stock | *Matthiola incana* | Full sun |
| | Stonecrop | *Sedum* | Full sun |
| | Strawberry | *Fragaria x ananassa* | Full sun |
| | Sunburst honey locust | *Gleditsia triacanthos inermis* | Full to part sun |
| | Sunflower | *Helianthus* | Full sun |
| | Sweet pea | *Lathyrus odoratus* | Full to part sun |
| | Tansy | *Tanacetum vulgare* | Full sun |

| | Common name | Latin name | Light |
|---|---|---|---|
| | Thistle | *Cirsium vulgare* | Full sun |
| | Thunbergia (Black-eyed Susan vine) | *Thunbergia alata* | Full sun |
| | Thyme | *Thymus* | Full sun |
| | Torenia | *Torenia fournieri* | Part sun to shade |
| | Trumpet vine | *Campsis radicans* | Full to part sun |
| | Tuberous begonia | *Begonia* x *tuber hybrida* | Full sun to shade |
| | Tulip | *Tulipa* | Full to part sun |

| | Common name | Latin name | Light |
|---|---|---|---|
| | Verbena | *Verbena* x *hybrida* | Full sun |
| | Vinca vine | *Vinca major* | Full sun to shade |
| | Viola | *Viola* x *wittrockiana* | Full sun to shade |
| | Virginia bluebells | *Mertensia virginica* | Part sun to shade |
| | Virginia creeper | *Parthenocissus quinquefolia* | Full to part sun |
| | Wax begonia | *Begonia* x *semperflorens-cultorum* | Full sun to shade |
| | Weeping birch | *Betula pendula* | Full sun |

| | Common name | Latin name | Light |
|---|---|---|---|
| | Weeping mulberry | *Morus alba* 'Pendula' | Full sun |
| | Weigela | *Weigela florida* | Full to part sun |
| | White clover | *Trifolium repens* | Full sun to shade |
| | Wisteria | *Wisteria sinensis* | Full sun |
| | Yew | *Taxus* | Full sun to shade |
| | Zinnia | *Zinnia elegans* | Full sun |
| | ZZ plant | *Zamioculcas kamiifolia* | Part sun to shade |

# Plants by Latin Name

| LATIN NAME | COMMON NAME |
|---|---|
| *Acer* | Maple |
| *Acer negundo* | Box elder |
| *Ageratum houstonianum* | Ageratum |
| *Ajuga reptans* | Bugleweed |
| *Alcea rosea* | Hollyhock |
| *Allium azureum* | Allium |
| *Allium schoenoprasum* | Chives |
| *Alyssum maritimum* | Alyssum |
| *Alyssum montanum* | Alyssum 'Mountain Gold' |
| *Amaranthus caudatus* | Amaranthus |
| *Amelanchier arborea* | Downy serviceberry |
| *Antirrhinum majus* | Snapdragon |
| *Aquilegia* | Columbine |
| *Aster* | Aster |
| *Astilbe* | Astilbe |
| *Azalea* | Azalea |
| *Begonia semperflorens* | Begonia |
| *Begonia x semperflorens-cultoru* | Wax begonia |
| *Begonia x tuber hybrida* | Tuberous begonia |
| *Bellis perennis* | English daisy |
| *Berberis* | Barberry |
| *Betula* | Birch |
| *Betula pendula* | Weeping birch |
| *Bougainvillea* | Bougainvillea |
| *Brassica oleracea* | Ornamental cabbage |
| *Brassica oleracea* | Ornamental kale |
| *Browallia* | Browallia |
| *Buddleia davidii* | Butterfly bush |
| *Buxus* | Boxwood |
| *Caladium* | Caladium |
| *Campanula medium* | Canterbury bells |
| *Campsis radicans* | Trumpet vine |
| *Canna* | Canna lily |

| LATIN NAME | COMMON NAME |
|---|---|
| *Centaurea cyanus* | Bachelor's button |
| *Chlorophytum comosum* | Spider plant |
| *Chrysanthemum sp.* | Mum |
| *Cirsium vulgare* | Thistle |
| *Clematis* | Clematis |
| *Cordyline indivisa* | Dracaena (spike) |
| *coreopsis* | Coreopsis |
| *Cornus* | Dogwood |
| *Corylus avellana 'Contorta'* | Corkscrew hazel |
| *Cosmos bipinnatus* | Cosmos |
| *Crocus* | Crocus |
| *Dahlia* | Dahlia |
| *Daphne* | Daphne |
| *Delphinium* | Delphinium (larkspur) |
| *Dianthus* | Dianthus |
| *Dicentra* | Bleeding heart |
| *Digitalis x mertonensis* | Foxglove |
| *Digitaria* | Crabgrass |
| *Echinacea* | Coneflower |
| *Euonymus fortunei* | Euonymus |
| *Festuca glauca* | Blue fescue |
| *Forsythia ovata* | Forsythia |
| *Fragaria x ananassa* | Strawberry plants |
| *Fritillaria imperialis* | Fritillaria |
| *Fuchsia* | Fuchsia |
| *Gladiolus* | Gladiolus |
| *Glechoma hederacea* | Creeping charlie |
| *Gleditsia* | Locust |
| *Gypsophila paniculata* | Baby's breath |
| *Hedera helix* | English Ivy |
| *Helianthus* | Sunflower |
| *Hemerocallis* | Day lily |
| *Heuchera* | Coral bells |

| LATIN NAME | COMMON NAME |
|---|---|
| Hibiscus rosa-sinensis | Hibiscus–tropical |
| Hibiscus syriacus | Rose of Sharon |
| Hosta | Hosta |
| Hyacinthus orientalis | Hyacinth |
| Hydrangea | Hydrangea |
| Hydrangea paniculata 'Limelight' | Hydrangea 'Limelight' |
| Iberis | Candytuft |
| Impatiens walleriana | Impatiens (busy lizzy) |
| Ipomoea nil | Morning glory |
| Iris sibirica | Iris–Siberian |
| Juniperus | Juniper |
| Lamium maculatum | Lamium (dead nettle) |
| Lathyrus odoratus | Sweet pea |
| Leucanthemum x superbum | Shasta daisy |
| Liatris spicata | Liatris |
| Lilium lancifolium | Asiatic lily |
| Lobelia erinu | Lobelia |
| Lupinus | Lupine |
| Magnolia x loebneri | Magnolia |
| Matteuccia struthiopteris | Ostrich fern |
| Matthiola incana | Stock |
| Medicago lupulina | Black medic |
| Mertensia virginica | Virginia bluebell |
| Morus alba 'Pendula' | Weeping mulberry |
| Myosotis sylvatica | Forget-me-not |
| Narcissus | Daffodil |
| Nemesia fruticans | Nemesia |
| Nerium oleander | Oleander |
| Nicotiana tabacum | Nicotiana |
| Ocimum basilicum | Basil |
| Origanum vulgare | Oregano |
| Osteospermum | Osteospermum (Cape daisy) |
| Paeonia | Peony |
| Papaver orientale | Oriental poppy |
| Parthenocissus quinquefolia | Virginia creeper |
| Parthenocissus tricuspidata | Boston ivy |

| LATIN NAME | COMMON NAME |
|---|---|
| Pelargonium | Geranium |
| Perovskia 'Filigran' | Sage (perennial) |
| Petroselinum crispum | Parsley |
| Petunia x hybrida | Petunia |
| Petunia x hybrida 'Wave' | Petunia 'Wave' |
| Philadelphus | Mock orange |
| Philodendron selloum | Philodendron |
| Phlox paniculata | Phlox |
| Picea | Spruce |
| Pinus | Pine |
| Plantago major | Broadleaf plantain |
| Potentilla fruticosa | Potentilla |
| Primula | Primrose (primula) |
| Prunus triloba plena | Flowering almond |
| Quercus | Oak |
| Rheum rhabarbarum | Rhubarb |
| Rhododendron spp | Rhododendron |
| Rosa | Rose |
| Rosmarinus officinalis | Rosemary |
| Rubus | Raspberry |
| Rudbeckia fulgida | Rudbeckia |
| Rudbeckia hirta | Black-eyed Susan |
| Salvia x sylvestris | Salvia |
| Salvia officinalis | Sage |
| Sambucus canadensis 'Laciniata' | Elderberry (lace shrub) |
| Sansevieria trifasciata | Snake plant |
| Schlumbergera | Christmas cactus |
| Scilla | Scilla |
| Sedum | Sedum |
| Sedum | Stonecrop |
| Senecio cineraria | Dusty miller |
| Solenostemon | Coleus |
| Sorbaria sorbifolia | False spirea |
| Spiraea x bumalda | Spirea |
| Stachys byzantina | Lamb's ear |
| Stellaria media | Chickweed |

| LATIN NAME | COMMON NAME |
| --- | --- |
| Syringa vulgaris | Lilac |
| Tagetes erecta | Marigold |
| Tanacetum vulgare | Tansy |
| Taxus | Yew |
| Thuja occidentalis | Cedar |
| Thunbergia | Thunbergia (black-eyed Susan vine) |
| Thymus | Thyme |
| Torenia fournieri | Torenia |
| Trifolium repens | White clover |
| Tropaeolum majus | Nasturtium |
| Tsuga canadensis | Hemlock |
| Tulipa | Tulip |
| Verbena x hybrida | Verbena |
| Viburnum lentago | Nannyberry |
| Vinca major | Vinca vine |
| Vinca minor | Periwinkle |
| Viola | Pansy |
| Viola x wittrockiana | Fall pansy |
| Weigela florida | Weigela |
| Wisteria sinensis | Wisteria |
| Zamioculcas zamiifolia | ZZ plant |
| Zinnia elegans | Zinnia |

# Index

Herbs
  bringing inside, 240–41
  in containers, 120, 134, 191
  harvesting, 189
  for poor soil, 97
Hibiscus, tropical, 118, 181, 303
Holland Marsh, 1
Hollyhock, 5, 82, 103, 105, 303
  and rust, 184
  staking, 154, 156
Honey locust, 177
Honeysuckle, 156–57
Horticultural lime, 9, 24
Hose, 249
  soaker, 57, 59, 161
Hosta, 4, 5, 52, 95, 303
  'Albopicta', 94
  'Elegans', 94
  slug-resistant varieties, 94
  and slugs, 179, 180
Hummingbirds, 168
Hyacinth, 83, 216, 219, 303
Hydrangea, 38, 156–57
  'Limelight', 235, 236, 303

**I**

Identifying plants, 4
Impatiens (busy lizzy), 5, 64, 86, 113, 114,
  118, 179, 211, 304
Indoor plants, 8, 277–79
  best place for, 280
  bringing indoors, 240–41
  humidity and, 280
  watering, 280
Insecticidal soap, 175, 177, 179, 186, 187
Insecticides, 139, 175, 179, 189
  biological, 124, 186

organic, 135, 186, 187
  systemic, 175
Insects, 86, 121, 123–25, 131, 133, 240
  ants, 173, 174, 186
  aphids, 124, 133, 149, 173, 175, 181, 186,
    187, 240
  beetles, 135–36, 175, 176, 177, 178, 186,
    187, 204
  beneficial, 181
  caterpillars, 82, 123–25, 186, 187
  chinch bugs, 203–04
  inspecting plants for signs of, 172, 173
  leaf miners, 174, 175
  mealybugs, 176, 177, 186
  protecting against, 136–38, 139, 172, 196
  scale insects, 177
  spider mites, 179, 186
  strawberry weevils, 135
  thrips, 179–80
  whiteflies, 131, 181, 186, 187
Intercropping, 194
Iris, 84, 92, 224, 304
Ivy, 118, 304
  Boston, 156, 177, 295
  English, 301

**J**

Japanese beetle, 175, 186, 204
Japanese maple, 247
Japanese silver grass, 235
June beetle, 175, 204
Juniper, 152, 177, 184, 235, 304
  spreading, 47

**K**

Kale, ornamental, 213, 215, 307

## L

Lace shrub, 47

Ladybugs, 136, 173, 177

Lamb's ear, 304

Lamium (dead nettle), 96, 97

Landscape designers, certified, 3

Landscape fabric, 57, 69, 130

    alternative, 61, 62

Larkspur. *See* Delphinium

Latin names of plants, 319–21

Lawn

    aerating, 26, 27, 267

    bulbs planted in, 216, 219

    chinch bugs in, 203–04

    dethatching, 23, 267, 268

    dog spots in, 24, 25

    early-spring checklist, 14

    eco-lawn mixes, 31

    fall checklist, 266

    fertilizing, 16, 17, 18, 28–29, 30, 143, 203, 269

    growing from seed, 15, 16–17, 266

    grubs in, 24, 204, 205

    laying sod, 15, 16, 18, 19–21

    mid- to late-spring checklist, 142

    mowing, 17, 18, 28, 142–43, 203, 267

    overseeding, 267

    repairing damage to, 24, 25, 26

    snow mould, 26, 267

    summer checklist, 203

    top-dressing, 26, 27, 267

    unsuitable areas for, 28

    watering, 19, 143, 203

    weed control, 14, 18, 31, 143, 144, 206, 267

Lawn mower, 28, 268

Leaf miner, 174, 175

Leaves, as compost and mulch, 219, 223, 224, 267, 269

Leek, 74

Lettuce, 68, 74, 134, 136, 194

Liatris, 304

Light, 7, 233

    full sun, 7

    indoor, 241, 280

    partial shade, 7

    partial sun, 7

    plant requirements, 293–316

    shade, 8

    for vegetable garden, 69, 74, 77

Lilac, 38, 103, 121, 122, 304

    powdery mildew on, 184

    pruning, 152, 153, 164

Lily, 219, 224

    Asiatic, 177, 293

Lily, Calla, 219

Lily, Canna, 84, 86, 87, 117, 118, 119, 219, 297

Lily, day, 5, 50, 52, 93, 94, 96, 300

Loam, 9, 10

Lobelia, 106, 109, 305

Locust, 305

    honey, 38, 177, 312

Love-lies-bleeding (amaranthus), 118, 293

Lupine, 92, 305

## M

Magnolia, 121, 177, 305

Mallow, 184

Manure

    composted, 43, 44, 62, 68, 76, 136

    fresh, 74

    green, 259

Maple, 5, 305

    sugar, 233, 236

Marigold, 5, 65, 131, 132, 133, 136, 137, 170, 173, 305

Pruning (cont.)

    paste, 38, 233

    roses, 99, 100–01, 152, 229

    shrubs, 38, 39, 103, 121, 122, 152, 164, 233

    spirea, 151

    tools for, 38, 39, 121

    trees, 38, 122, 136, 233

Pumpkin, 127, 254

Pyrethrin, 187

## R

Rabbits, 135, 199, 201, 247

Raccoons, 24

Radish, 68, 74, 134, 136, 194

Rain barrel, 160, 162

Raised bed, 9, 69, 72–73

Rakes, 23, 271

Raspberry, 38, 68, 77, 309

Red lily beetle, 177, 178

Retaining walls, 47

Rhizomes, 84, 85

Rhododendron, 5, 9, 44, 163, 223, 245, 309

    importance of deadheading, 152

Rhubarb, 68, 75, 76, 102, 199, 259, 262, 309

Rodents, 247

Roof overhangs, 165

Root rot, 44, 45, 164

Root(s)

    ball, 52, 54, 57

    damage to, 164

    fertilizer and, 62, 64, 136, 157

    judging quality of plants by, 86, 89

    mulching to protect, 62, 231

    watering and, 8, 59, 62, 136, 157, 160, 161, 196, 229

Rose, 310

    blackspot-resistant varieties, 183

    Canadian Explorer, 99

    David Austin, 99

    deadheading, 152

    fertilizing, 99, 152

    Flower Carpet, 99

    hips, 229

    hybrid tea, 99

    pruning, 99, 100–01, 152, 229

    and rust, 184

    standard (tree), 99, 229

    watering, 99

    winterizing, 229–31

Rosemary, 191, 310

Rose of Sharon, 121, 310

Rotenone, 187

Rudbeckia, 310

Rue, 201

Rust, 184, 185, 187

## S

Sage, 173, 310

Salt, sidewalk and road, 245

Salvia, 108, 111, 118, 311

Sand, 8, 9, 10, 44, 46, 47

Sap beetle, 135–36

Scale insects, 177, 178

Scarecrows, 199

Scilla, 216, 221, 310

Sedum, 52, 93, 97, 98, 215, 311

    'Autumn Joy', 97

    'Blue Spruce', 213

    'Brilliant', 213

Seed

    bird-, 238

    catalogues, 277

    collecting from annuals, 223, 225

    growing plants from, 65, 277